MASTER
SUCCESS

Create a life of purpose, passion,
peace and prosperity

Bill FitzPatrick
The American Success Institute
a nonprofit organization

MASTER SUCCESS ™, 100 ACTION PRINCIPLES OF THE SHAOLIN ™, POSITIVE MENTAL ATTITUDES ™, AFRICAN-AMERICANS ON SUCCESS ™, SPORTS LEGENDS ON SUCCESS ™, WINNING WITH SMALL BUSINESS ™, TENGA UNA ACTITUD MENTAL POSITIVA ™, WOMEN ON SUCCESS ™, and ATTITUDES MENTALES POSITIVES ™ are all trademarks of the American Success Institute, Inc.

Educational and motivational materials from the American Success Institute are available at special discounts for bulk purchases. For additional information, contact:

American Success Institute
5 North Main Street
Natick, MA 01760

www.MasterSuccess.com

Phone: 1-800-585-1300

e-mail: asi@MasterSuccess.com

Book design, typography, and electronic pagination by Painted Turtle Productions, Newton, MA.

Printed in the United States of America

ISBN 1-884864-12-0
Library of Congress Catalog Card Number: 99-95536

TABLE OF CONTENTS

WHAT OTHERS SAY
ABOUT
THE ACTION PRINCIPLES

...a positive and informative book of basic life principles to survive and succeed. From children to grown-ups, from the impoverished to the wealthy, there is something in there for everyone.
Kirk Fordice, Governor of Mississippi

This eminently readable book goes a long way toward providing the reader with answers to their daily challenges in attaining goals for themselves and their families.
General Stanley W. Wisnioski, Jr. (MSG, Retired)

Congratulations on your success and national recognition for offering free business education on the Internet. On behalf of the people of Guam, I wish you the best of luck in all your endeavors.
Carl T.C. Gutierrez, Governor of Guam

What a great little book! It's easy to carry around and one can refer to it at any time.
US Representative Cliff Stearns

Having a copy of this means a great deal to me and will certainly come in handy. It will have a special place in my library.
US Senator Michael B. Enzi

A wonderful addition to my collection.
E. Benjamin Nelson, Governor of Nebraska

This book is thoughtful and hard hitting, and if you follow through will lead you to a better life.
Bill Rogers, Olympian

A great inspirational guide for daily living and personal success.
Dan R. Bannister, CEO DynCorp

Really good stuff.
James J. Howard, CEO, Northern States Power

It impresses me as a useful quick reference guide for personal and business use.
David L. Squier, CEO, Howmet Corp.

Very interesting, informative and helpful.
Manuel Avendando, Managing Editor, El Diario La Prensa

Congratulations. Common sense values condensed in an easy read.
Gerald Lestina, CEO, Roundy's Corp.

Packs a wealth of wisdom for life.
Dr. Robert Doherty

I will keep re-reading the book. It is a great guide to happiness and success.
Dean L. Buntrock, CEO, WMX Technologies

A helpful and informative book...with the capacity to assist me in my public as well as my private life.
US Senator John Ashcroft

MASTER
SUCCESS

*Create a life of purpose, passion,
peace and prosperity*

INTRODUCTION

If we did all the things we are capable of doing,
we would literally astonish ourselves.
Thomas Edison, American inventor (b. 1847)

This may be one of the most rewarding books you will ever read.

In the years to come you may look back on this day as a turning point in your life. Indeed this very moment might be the moment of decision, when you began setting a new course for your life; when you decided to master your life rather than your life mastering you. Let this be the moment when everything changed.

Master Success is a total, life affirming system for those willing to do the work to have it all. It's a rewarding career, a loving family, true friends, respect in the community, plenty of money and the inner peace that comes from doing your best. You can have all of it. The Master Success System is based on 100 Action Principles which can change your life. You will soon find the personal power of the Action Principles. The choice to seize and use this power is yours. Forever changed, you need never look back. Your spirit will soar.

The Master Success System isn't for those looking for quick fixes, undiscovered secrets or rewards without effort. It isn't for wimps. It is for those who dare to act. It is for those who want to be in the game and not sitting on the sidelines. It is choosing to make your life an exciting adventure. It is going as far as you can with all that you have. No one is selecting you to become successful. You are selecting yourself. You are accepting a self-imposed regime of hard work and service to others. Everyone will not choose this challenge. Most will not choose this challenge. The Master Success System will deliver a shock to any complacency you may harbor. Can you do it? Yes. Will you do it? This is the question we must each answer. Your life is at stake.

By electing to follow the Master Success System, you are choosing to be tough. Tough means that you are willing to stand tall and persevere. Even when your mind and body signal perfectly good reasons for giving up, you go on.

Tough is a soldier willing to be courageous in battle. This tough is obvious. But tough can be seen every day if we choose to look. Tough may be a patient undergoing chemotherapy or a single mother struggling to raise children. Tough may be a business owner who loses everything and quietly begins again or a young adult who must sacrifice to care for an elderly parent. Tough can be an alcoholic ready to face rehab or an athlete living in a wheelchair. Tough can be rejecting false praise and honestly accepting you and your children for who and what you are. Tough is an ability to make the best from what you are given. Tough is making the decision to replace whining and dependence with self-reliance, independence and action.

Being tough can take you a long way.

You've got to be tough to do the big things in life like taking risks, admitting mistakes, and changing bad habits. You've got to be tough to do the little things like biting your tongue, waiting your turn and suffering fools. Self-reliance and self-confidence will demand your toughness.

Then, you must temper toughness with kindness. You've got to be kind to receive the big blessings in life like inner peace and respect. You've got to be kind to receive the daily blessings like a loving life partner, true friends, compatible co-workers and well-behaved children. Many times it will be tough to be kind. You will be kind anyway.

The Master Success System will lead you to prosperity. This is the easy part. If you are tough and kind, money naturally flows toward you. You don't have to become entangled in intricate financial plans. You don't have to become a workaholic. The style and attitudes you develop from adhering to the Action Principles will be more than you need to acquire everything you want.

Few older people look back on their lives and wish that they had worked longer hours and made more money. This system can make you rich. In fact, it can make you very rich. However, greed is not the spirit or intent of the system. The Master Success System defines financial independence in terms of the life enhancing possibilities that money brings. If you are self-

2

centered and selfish, no one is going to care if you have a lot of money or live in a big house or drive a luxury car. In fact, you will more likely be resented than befriended. The intent of the system is to show you how to have the financial resources necessary to live comfortably, to take special care of those you love, to help others and to have the free time to develop your individual, God given talents. Yes, you are talented. Too many people are pressured and stressed by modern life to find extra minutes in their days to finish the ordinary work they have to do. You will be an exception. You will find the time to identify and develop your extraordinary talents.

You will have the time. You will have the money. Commit your will to mastering success.

When you are tough, you are dedicated to self-improvement and the idea of challenging yourself to do your best. You will not be afraid to build upon and defend your values. This tough attitude could make you a better employee, better business owner, or better investor. You'll be better all the time at all aspects of your career. You naturally rise to the top of whatever endeavors you choose. You become a leader.

When you are kind, you are focused on the people around you: co-workers, employees, your superiors, customers and the friends of your customers. You listen to them. You ask for their advice. You help them out. You share the credit. You make them look good. You ask for their business and they give it to you willingly. You ask for their testimonials and they gladly become your ambassadors, praising your selfless attitude to increasingly wider audiences. When you live according to the Action Principles, you start a mutually rewarding cycle of giving and receiving. As you show generosity, you will find how frequently others wish to reciprocate with a compliment, a helping hand, a raise, a promotion or more business.

In writing the Action Principles and putting together the Master Success System, I looked back over a half century of my own life. Who influenced me?

I can remember as a little boy reading the Horatio Alger books about penniless newsboys. They later became business tycoons. As a teenager, I read Dale Carnegie, Norman Vincent Peale and Napoleon Hill. I continue to read, enjoy and learn from Tony Robbins, Les Brown and Stephen Covey to name just a few. I owe a debt to these and many other past and present motivators.

I worked my way through college as the Assistant Manager of Customer Service at Sears and as a Sergeant in the Army Reserve. Immediately after college, I went to graduate school at Boston College where I majored in special education and met Dougie. Dougie, along with Mario, Don and John were to play influential roles in directing the course my life has taken. Each of these men had important lessons to teach me. I am blessed to have known them and to have understood their messages.

I met Dougie during my student teaching internship. Dougie was a 17-year-old dwarf and the school's most popular student. He was a hell raiser. He raced wheelchairs. He dueled with crutches. He made phony PA announcements. He smoked cigarettes in the boys' room and joked about smoking not stunting his growth. In a school where the atmosphere could so easily have been ruled by gloom and depression, there was joy and laughter because of this one extraordinary young man. Everybody loved him. Dougie chose to live his life out front and exposed without worrying about what every person thought of him. Teachers or administrators didn't intimidate him. He chose to have fun. Every minute of every day, he was committed to making his life an exciting adventure. You could see him thinking, *"What can I do next to have some fun?"* I'm sure that Dougie was well aware of his life expectancy and decided to live every day that he had. Dougie died in his early twenties. I learned from Dougie what it means to be courageous and to enjoy each and every day.

For fifteen years, I ran a high school program for young men with court problems. My classroom was basically a revolving door of getting jobs for kids with large companies who hired them for the public relations benefits. Usually, a kid would work at one place for a few months, get fired and move on to the next job. This revolving door of jobs seemed like the way it was always going to be. Then one day I got a new student, Mario.

Mario proceeded to tell me that he appreciated my offer of help in getting a job but that he didn't want it. He told me that the jobs that I got for people weren't his style – hired, fired, hired, fired. He had been thinking that he wanted to start his own business. Of course, I immediately brushed off his plan by informing him that someone can't just decide to start his or her

4

own business. I told him that you need a business plan and financing and training and experience. Naturally, Mario proved me wrong.

Mario started a handyman service. Without a moment of hesitation, he knocked on one door after another. He cleaned basements and washed windows and raked and polished and fixed. He went from one satisfied customer to another. He had many customers. As he'd finish one job, the homeowner would be ready to give him another. His services became in such demand he had several other kids in the class working for him. I asked him why he was never afraid to knock on a stranger's door and ask for work. He said, *"Why should I be afraid, Bill? Lots of people need all kinds of work done around their houses. I do a good job. I don't charge too much. I even give the old people a little break. Bill, you're not considering that most of these people have kids and grandkids who are too (blank blank) lazy to help them. People really need a worker like me."* From Mario, I learned to be a man of action. Stop worrying and making excuses and get to work. If you are willing to do a good job, don't be afraid to knock on doors and say so.

At 21, I bought a three-family house with an attached barn both as a residence and as an investment property. I settled in for the long haul. Then, I got a call from Don, the broker who had sold me the house, telling me that he had a buyer for the property. I told Don that I had no intention of selling. He told me to reconsider because he had the perfect buyer for my property willing to pay top dollar. It was an extended family and the father also wanted a space to open a small machine shop. To get rid of Don and his crazy scheme, I told him twice the price that I had paid for the property. He negotiated the sale and a nice profit for me. In fact, being a high school teacher, it would have taken me two years to earn that same amount of money. To me, Don was a genius.

With my profit, Don wanted me to buy both a six-family and a single-family house. I said, *"Yeah, but, Don, I really don't want to get involved with all those tenants."* Don replied, *"Bill, love all those tenants. These are people who actually want to give you money. Listen, finding people who want to give you money is what business is all about. Since you haven't got much money, you'll borrow lots of money but you aren't going to have to pay it back. You are going to have these wonderful people called ten-*

ants who, every month, are going to give you money to pay back everything that you borrow. You borrow money and tenants pay the money back. This is the easiest simplest best business in the world. This is the real estate investment business."

I made real estate investing my part-time business. From Don, I did learn to value my tenants who were paying my mortgages while the properties appreciated. It was a good business and is a good business. You will learn much more about real estate in this book and on the MasterSuccess.com website.

By my late twenties, enjoying married life a little too much, I had ballooned up to 230 pounds on my wife's gourmet cooking. I needed a new challenge. I wanted something physical that would get me back in shape. Since I was working with juvenile offenders, karate seemed like a good choice.

That first day of martial arts training, I squeezed into a very tight white uniform with a stiff white belt that barely made it around my waist. I looked much more comical than menacing.

My instructor for the next seven years was John. He was a Shaolin Kempo karate master.

I clearly remember that John treated me with respect that first day. Years later when I was a black belt, he showed me the same respect. John treated everyone the same. He liked people. John made every person feel important every day. From crying six-year-olds to trophy oriented teens, from the shy to the macho, John took a minute to talk to everyone every day. You never had a doubt that John was your friend and he just happened to run a very profitable martial arts business. John's retention rate for students was amazingly high. His attitude toward business was simple, *"Strangers aren't going to give me any money. I've only got my students to pay me. I'd better be nice to them."*

I have met many people with pieces of paper that said that they were MBAs, Masters in Business Administration. Without the paper, John was a master in business administration.

For years, I thought that the real estate business was special. I thought that it was only in real estate that you could borrow money and have others pay those loans back for you. I was wrong. John taught me that in any business, it is your students, customers, clients, and patients. It is people and only people who are going to give you the money to have everything that you ever wanted in your life for yourself and your family. If you focus on the people who are giving you money, you will make more money. From John, I learned that personality and kindness pay big dividends in business and in life.

I started the American Success Institute in 1994 after a brief educational trip to Russia. My role was as both a chaperone and a teacher of American history. The Russian students weren't particularly interested in American history. However, after I mentioned my business background they seemed very interested in learning about getting rich. Almost all of the kids had small part-time businesses and they all wanted to make lots of money like Americans. Their enthusiasm for success was contagious and inspired me. On the long plane ride home, I couldn't let the idea go. What if American kids had this same enthusiasm for success? What if everyone had this enthusiasm for success? I wanted to write down my ideas and see what developed. And, here you have it. It is yours. The books, the courses, websites, seminars are yours.

The American Success Institute is a 501(c)3 nonprofit organization. This means that our emphasis is placed on helping you achieve success and not on our perks and salaries. This means that you never need to spend another cent to enjoy the core benefits of the system. All the other courses and books associated with the Master Success System are either free or optional supplements to this book. If you choose, you can help us help others by buying and distributing additional copies of this book to family, friends and through worthwhile social agencies in your community. In any book order, the cost of the first book is always $19.95 and the cost of all additional copies is always $10.00. Order on the website at MasterSuccess.com or by calling 1-800-585-1300. Thank you in advance for doing all that you can.

As a martial arts master, my obligation is to study, practice and teach. By definition and by personal choice, it is a simple life. My goal is to pass on what was given to me by Dougie, Mario, Don, John and many others. The websites,\ MasterSuccess.com and Dojo.com are my teaching tools. My writing style is a blend of Shaolin Kempo karate master, Army Sergeant and teacher of teenage court offenders. It is direct. It is declarative. Most of this material does present a clear choice. You choose to do it. You choose not to do it. Your life is your personal journey. You make your own choices. You can choose to work at a personal mastery level. You can choose to master success.

The heart of *Master Success* is the 100 Action Principles. Refer to them often as you formulate your own ideas and plans. The message of the Action Principles is simple; improve yourself and help others. It is a business message. It is a martial arts message. It is a human message.

If, each day, you've thought about who you are, where you are and how you can become a better person, you will find prosperity beyond your expectations. Your manner will be self-confident. Your attitude will be positive. Your body will be strong. Your mind will be calm. Your fears will be few. If, each day, your focus at home, work, play and in the community has been on helping others, you will find peace beyond your expectations. Those who raised you will be proud of you. Your guidance will be remembered and your leadership sought. Your personal encounters will be joyful and your friendships many. Your value to society will be great. Believe in the power of always trying to lead an exemplary life. As Gandhi said, *"My life is my message."* Choose to make your life your message.

Let this be your moment. Now is your time. There is no other. Let's share a common goal to live quality lives. Let's find a purpose for our lives that we can follow with passion. Yes, we want to be financially independent. Yes, we want good health. Yes, we want strong bonds to family and friends. Yes, we can become tough, kind and rich and have it all. We are choosing to make or not make that decision right now.

Following the Master Success System, you will be changed immediately and forever. You will realize that you are the Master Piece.

Then, let's begin to Master Success.

Bill

CHAPTER ONE
MASTER SUCCESS 1

There is more in us than we know. If we can be made to see it, perhaps, for the rest of our lives we will be unwilling to settle for less.
Kurt Hahn, Founder, Outward Bound (b. 1886)

In the introduction, we told you that reading this book may be a turning point in your life. You may think that such moments cannot happen, or that they only happen to other people. Yet they do happen, all the time.

You may think that years of education or therapy or training or meditation are necessary to achieve real change. But how long does it take to go from being sad to being happy? In the right situation it can happen in a split second. You are angry about a situation at work and you unexpectedly see someone you love and the anger disappears and you are filled with happiness. You are depressed and you receive good news and all of a sudden you can barely remember why you had been so down. Or it can go the other way. You are happy and then someone cuts you off in traffic and suddenly you are upset.

Your mind changes constantly. It is highly adaptive. Simple changes in the way that you think can make the difference between fulfillment and misery. We've all seen people who have everything we think is necessary for success and yet seemed to be depressed. Then we've seen others who, we would think, have every reason to be unhappy and yet seem to be joyous and full of life. What is the difference between those who can never find reasons for happiness and those who almost never see a reason for sadness? The difference is in how and what they think. The Russian author Anton Chekov wrote, *"Man is what he believes."* If you can learn the principles and strategies of the successful you can use their methods to

Anton Chekov

9

achieve whatever you desire.

The key is to take control of your own mind. You are about to learn about the tremendous power of self-control and self-

reliance. These are inner resources, which you already possess, which you have always possessed. You may not have realized that you have these abilities. You may not have used them or you may have underutilized them. This is all about to change. After taking the actions recommended in this book and following the Action Principles, get ready to hear yourself described as outstanding, extraordinary and

Thomas Carlyle respected as well as tough, kind and rich. Get ready for peace and prosperity. Get ready to live a life of conviction and purpose. The Scottish essayist Thomas Carlyle wrote, *"Have a purpose in life, and throw yourself into your work with all the strength of mind and muscle as God has given."* Life is your game to win. Life should be about growth and your willingness to keep learning and to keep helping others. What are you prepared to give, to sacrifice, to endure? Are you ready? Dr. Abraham Maslow, one of the founders of humanistic psychology, wrote *"If you plan on being anything less than*

Dr. Abraham Maslow *you are capable of being, you will probably be unhappy all the days of your life."*

THE POWER TO CHOOSE

You have the power to choose; to choose good over evil; to choose joy over sadness; to choose a fun-filled life over loneliness; to choose independence over dependency, to choose inner peace over depression. You can choose prosperity. You can choose healthy living. You can choose your career, your house, your car, and your life partner. You can choose to be a positive role model for your children, employees, neighbors and co-workers. You can choose for yourself or you can allow time and circumstance to choose for you. You have free will. Realize that the power to control comes from the power to choose. Life brings you hundreds and thousands of choices to make. You will make them every day. Be prepared to choose love and self-respect and high achievement and service and inner peace.

The Indian mystic Patanjali, who lived several hundred years before Christ, and who first recognized the power in the practice of meditation, said, *"When you are inspired by some great purpose, some extraordinary project, all your thoughts break their bonds; your mind transcends limitations, your consciousness expands in every direction, and you find yourself in a new, great and wonderful world. Dormant forces, faculties and talents become alive, and you discover yourself to be a greater person by far than you ever dreamed yourself to be."*

ACCEPT PERSONAL RESPONSIBILITIES

Your preparation for success is not necessarily about a wall of degrees earned from years of formal education. It could be. But much more important is whether you were a serious student or just taking up space in a succession of meaningless classes. Whether your education is formal or informal doesn't matter as much as your determination to become self-educated. You are responsible for you. Your mother and father can't make you educated. Your teachers can't make you educated. You must make you educated. You can read and learn anything you want. Go to the library. Log onto the Internet. Start learning and never stop.

Don't listen to ridiculous theories or the pressure of self-interested groups that want to pigeon hole you into believing that for some reason you are a member of a group that needs special quotas or special handouts to succeed. You don't. Success is not about your ancestry, birth order, gender, family money, creed, color, sexual preference or the movement of the stars. It is about your personal individual commitment to goal attainment through consistent positive action. Want it. Do it. Do it for yourself and for those you love.

FOLLOW THE ACTION PRINCIPLES

Everything about the Master Success System keeps returning to the Action Principles. Let the Action Principles be your guide. Sometimes read them through in order. Sometimes read them randomly. Think about each one. You will find that you can use the Action Principles to succeed at anything – making money, finding inner peace, raising children, finding a life partner, or whatever else you can imagine. The Action Principles are now yours. The Action Principles are nothing without you. By committing to the Action Principles, you will see opportunities abound around you. You will immediately feel successful. This will be the powerful new you!

How fast can this begin to happen?

It's in less time than it has taken you to read this chapter.

You may find it hard to believe that change can happen that quickly. But it does. In the blink of an eye a smoker can become a non-smoker. A naysayer can become a can-do optimist. In a second a lazy person can become a hard worker. A coward can become courageous.

How does it happen?

That is what you will learn in the pages to come.

Unlike most books that you just sit back and read, this book is part of a system. The system is meant to be understood and acted upon. This is life's journey. Don't anticipate being happy in ten years. Be happy right now. Right now, you can choose to become fitness oriented, hard working and kind to others. Right now, you can define success based on your own values and beliefs. Make the choice. You don't need anyone's permission. Peace and prosperity await your choice.

Theodore Roosevelt

ORDINARY PEOPLE CAN LEAD EXTRAORDINARY LIVES

Here is an excerpt from a speech that the American president Theodore Roosevelt gave early in the 20th century, *"There are two kinds of success. One is the very rare kind that comes to the man who has the power to do what no one else has the power to do. That is genius. But the average man who wins what we call success is not a genius. He is a man who has merely the ordinary qualities that he shares with his fellows, but who has developed those ordinary qualities to a more than ordinary degree."*

In the next chapter, you'll find a list of qualities characteristic of mankind's most successful people. These are characteristics which you can copy. As you begin to identify and develop these characteristics for yourself, you will grow increasingly enthusiastic and energized as incredible personal opportunities emerge. You will begin to see new ways to make real changes in your life. The Irish playwright George Bernard Shaw pointed out, *"Progress is impossible without change, and those who cannot change their minds cannot change anything."* Quite possibly these changes are greater and more exciting than any you have ever made.

How much change is possible? How much success is possible?

George Bernard Shaw

To find out what is possible you need only look at history. You only have to read the quotes sprinkled throughout the text. Successful living is not a new concept. There have always been successful people in every age and from every country. There have always been people of influence and fortune. Every page of history shows us individuals who made decisions to lead extraordinary lives and become generals, politicians, explorers, composers, builders, inventors and merchants. The style, attitude and habits that these people used to succeed are exactly the same that you can use. If someone else has done it before then you know that it can be done again. Why not by you?

Henry Ford was not a character in a novel. He was a real man who changed the world. George Washington existed. He took action. Because he and the other men and women who founded the World's democracies took action you may be lucky enough to live in a country where you can enjoy incredible prosperity and freedom.

Some might say that is in the past and that those sort of things don't happen anymore.

They are wrong.

Right now there are men and women doing things that will change the world. These are things that will bring them more wealth than has ever been possible in the history of mankind. They will help bring peace and happiness to mankind. They represent every race, every creed and every age. Some are born to poverty and others to privilege. Some live in perfect health while others by birth or accident are physically challenged. Some emerge from supportive, loving environments while others have had to fend for themselves. All have decided to live their lives as tough, compassionate people of action. On the journey to peace and prosperity, they have committed themselves to self-improvement and service to others. This is the good life. Theirs will be proud, meaningful lives. This can be your life.

If you have had an easy life and have had everything handed

to you and seen everything always go your way, you are at a disadvantage. You may have to be diligent in your efforts to overcome the well meaning pampering of your parents and teachers. Your spirit may be soft. Your ability to fully appreciate the small joys and victories of daily life may have been taken from you. If you have had to work hard and struggle and put up with a few unpleasant things, you may be better prepared to meet the challenges and enjoy the blessings ahead. The cadets at West Point are motivated by the following maxim which is good advice for anyone willing to work for success, *"Risk more than others think is safe. Care more than others think is wise. Dream more than others think is practical. Expect more than others think is possible."*

OPPORTUNITIES ABOUND

There has never been a time with more opportunity than there is today. This holds true regardless of where you are or what the economy is doing. Right now businesses have access to better technology, more information and greater markets than they have had at any other time. Consumers have more purchasing power to spend on the products and services being provided by the millions of new businesses being started each year. At the same time those products create new opportunities for millions of new businesses by providing affordable tools that the millionaires of the future can use to make their dreams realities.

"Come on, Louis. No risk, no reward."

It is possible that you, the person reading this sentence right now, could be one of the people who will take advantage of these incredible opportunities and help build a better life and a better world. You can make the choice to pledge allegiance to action.

When we say that change is possible instantly does this mean that you can become head of Ford Motor Company in five minutes? Of course not. But you can quickly start down the path that can lead you to success and fulfillment every bit as great as that achieved by Henry Ford. You can be happy. You can be content that you have done your best.

Too many people look at where they are and imagine that this is where they must always be. They feel somehow trapped by the status quo. They look at the people who have what they want and think that those people were somehow lucky or blessed.

This overlooks all of the things that people have overcome to be where they are. If you look at the rich you may admire all the exterior trappings of their wealth. You cannot see the rocky path they may have walked to arrive at financial success. If you could look inside their hearts and minds, you might be surprised to find the many obstacles they have overcome. Perhaps there were obstacles far greater than you face. You might also be surprised to discover that despite all they overcame they succeeded using simple, practical principles. Remember that it's not where you start that counts but the joys you experience along the path. Over the next few weeks as you read and think about what you have read, you will learn these same simple, practical principles. You will learn by doing as you complete the assignments at the end of each chapter.

Epictetus

You may still be thinking *'Yes, I know all that but you don't understand. I have really serious problems. I just can't do it.'* In the first century, the Greek philosopher Epictetus addressed similar concerns, *"It is difficulties that show what men are made of."* If you say that you can't do it, the world will believe you. If you say that you can do it, the world will await the proof.

MEET THE CHALLENGES

There are many reasons you might feel that you cannot succeed. You may feel you are too shy to do it.

In 1965 Jim Morrison and Ray Manzarek were trying to get their new band, The Doors, started by playing in small clubs around LA. There were just two problems – the audiences hated them and Morrison couldn't face the audience. It was much more than being nervous or reluctant to go onstage. He literally could not face the audience while he was performing. He would sing while facing the blank wall at the back of the stage giving the audience a clear view of the back of his head!

To avoid this embarrassing scene, Ray would do most of the singing. Yet, Ray knew that it was Morrison who was blessed with the extraordinary singing talent. It was Morrison's voice that could turn around the hostility of the crowds. Ray was certain that if he kept pestering Morrison to connect and keep practicing that they would eventually find their audience and success.

When Ray and Jim met in 1964, Morrison had never sung in a band. Morrison did listen to Ray. He did keep practicing. By taking action, night after night and exercising little bits of courage, he was able slowly to overcome his fear and became an incredible stage performer able to bring stadiums full of cheering people to their feet.

You may feel you are not educated enough to do it.

Bill Gates dropped out of Harvard to go into business writing computer software.

Winston Churchill graduated last in his college class.

Elvis got an F in music.

Les Brown, the great motivational speaker, was labeled *"educable mentally retarded"* in grade school.

Muriel Seibert was the first woman to make one billion dollars and she only had a high school diploma.

Richard Branson of Virgin Airlines, with a net worth estimated at $1.9 billion, dropped out of high school.

Stephen Spielberg was an unknown C student in high school.

Thomas Edison had only three months of formal education.

Sean Connery quit school at age 13 with a sixth grade education. One of his early jobs was polishing coffins. His first acting coach told him that he needed more schooling. That day, he picked up a book and started reading and has never stopped.

What separated these people from the crowd was not credentials from exclusive schools or rich parents or knowing the right people but rather a commitment to setting goals and then taking decisive action every day to achieve them. Study and keep studying. Read a book that leads to the next book. Ask a question that leads to the next question. Again, ultimately, all education is self-education. Start today. Never stop.

You may feel you are not healthy enough to do it.

Glenn Cunningham's legs were burned so badly that he was told that he would never walk again. He won an Olympic gold medal in track.

Max Cleland stepped on a mine in Vietnam and lost an arm and two legs. He went on to become the youngest person to administer the U.S. Veterans Administration and was the first Vietnam veteran to head the agency. He is now a United States Senator.

Eddie Timanus lost his eyesight to retinoblastoma tumors at age 2. He became a sports reporter for USA Today and a champion on the TV quiz show Jeopardy.

Robert Kerrey received massive permanent injuries while completing his mission and saving the lives of the Navy Seal team under his command in Vietnam. Lt. Kerrey was awarded the Congressional Medal of Honor. He is now a United States Senator.

As a child, Wilma Rudolph caught pneumonia and scarlet fever leaving her with a crippled left leg. She later won three Olympic gold medals in track.

Helen Keller was blind and deaf. She became a teacher, a writer and an inspiration to millions.

Jackie Joyner-Kersee came from an impoverished background. Her family life was traumatic. Her mother died. She had asthma. Yet she has won seven Olympic medals.

Heather Whitestone is deaf and yet became the 1995 Miss America.

Professional quarterbacks complete only 60% of their passes. Basketball players hit only 50% of their shots. Baseball players only hit 25% of the time.

Perhaps you feel that circumstances are against you.

Country superstar Shania Twain grew up poor. At 22, her parents were killed in a car crash. Her first CD bombed. Her second sold 9 million copies.

Nelson Mandela spent 30 years in prison before becoming the president of South Africa.

Tommy Hilfiger started his business by selling jeans from the trunk of his car.

In 1962, Decca Records wouldn't give the Beatles a recording contract.

Twenty-three publishers rejected Theodore Geisel, *"Dr. Seuss,"* before his first book was accepted.

Tom Clancy worked for many years as a low level defense analyst before becoming a mega-selling author.

Ruth Fertel had two small boys and a low paying job when her husband left. She mortgaged her house to start a small restaurant. Her chain of Ruth's Chris Steak Houses is now nationally respected.

Ray Kroc was fifty-two when he bought the McDonald brothers' hamburger stand and Colonel Sanders began his chain when he was in his mid-sixties.

In 1945, just seven weeks after the end of World War Two, Masaru Ibuka and seven employees rented a small section of a bombed-out department store and set up the headquarters of the Tokyo Telecommunications Research Institute in the shattered ruins of the city's old shopping district. They had no heat and the employees had to scavenge for food. The company's first consumer product was an electrically heated cushion that was a fire hazard. Their first successful consumer product was a phonograph player. There were terrible shortages of basic materials and the engineers had to salvage the steel needed from the structural reinforcements of demolished buildings.

Starting from a bombed out building in the rubble of postwar Tokyo Masaru Ibuka persisted in the face of failed products, shortages of materials, foot-dragging government bureaucrats, skeptical American partners and wary American consumers and in just twelve years revolutionized – indeed practically created – the field of consumer microelectronics. You know his company as Sony Electronics.

Ibuka epitomized the spirit of the Action Principles. He was persistent. Despite numerous false starts he remained fully committed to his dream of creating consumer products. He was totally committed to serving the customer. When others chose the easy money and safety of government contracts he pursued the consumer market by coming to the United States and personally studying American consumer needs. He was committed to constant and never-ending improvement and the highest standards of quality. He wrote a mission statement and then acted to carry it out each and every day.

COMBINE ATTITUDE WITH ACTION

You may think that achievements like these are only done by special people, better people. But what makes those who achieve greatness excel isn't necessarily extraordinary talent or brains or aptitude but rather the fact that they are willing to go out and do something with what they have got. It is attitude. It is action. French President Charles De Gaulle encouraged his people with these words, *"Nothing great will ever be achieved without great men, and men are great only if they are determined to be so."*

Charles De Gaulle

WHAT IF YOU CHOOSE NOT TO GO FOR IT?

What if it is just too much trouble? You just can't be bothered. There are bills to pay. Your friends wouldn't approve. Better to just stay where you are. Many find a comforting cocooning quality in the status quo. No one will think less of you. It's not like you ever really could have made it.

You can tell yourself all that now. And it might provide some small comfort, for the time being. But how will you feel in ten years when you look around and many of the people you know who made a different decision, who did take action and who did take control of their futures are now reaping the rewards while you remain forever the same. Maybe you'll be a little bit better off, making a few thousand more dollars a year or perhaps with a few more possessions. But not where you wish you could be. You won't be where you could have been. Not who you might have been.

Even now you can look back at those actions not taken, those things not said, those dreams abandoned and feel the pain of loss. There is the pain of knowing what you gave up, the pain of knowing that giving up was a choice and that you are responsible for that choice. If that is bad, why willingly subject yourself to another year of inaction? After another two years? After ten? Think of ten years of shattered dreams, or ten years of missed opportunities. What price are you paying today for decisions that you made in the past? Mark Twain echoed this sentiment in saying, *"Twenty years from now you will be more disappointed by the things you didn't do than by the ones*

Mark Twain

you did. So throw off the bowlines, sail away from the safe harbor. Catch the trade winds in your sails. Explore. Dream."

MAKE THE NEXT YEARS YOUR BEST

Now think about ten years of being your best. Free yourself from all self-imposed limits and fears. Be in control of your own life, constantly improving yourself and helping others. Make your highest vision of yourself a reality. Imagine your entire life transformed. Think of what you will do for the people you love. Imagine the possibilities. Think of those things that you have always wished you could have but you decided they were out of your reach. Think of those things you always wanted to accomplish but you decided you just weren't good enough to do them. What will it be like to have had those things, to do those things, for ten years? Think of all the experiences you will have had. You'll have ten years of incredible excitement and pleasure and ten years of making your dreams come true.

As you read this book and take the recommended actions, you will find yourself at a crossroads in your life. Which path will you take? Will it be action or inaction? If you finish reading the book, there is little doubt that you will make the correct initial choice. Everyone has 24/7, no more no less. You have the

same amount of time to do with your life as Henry Ford, Shakespeare and George Washington. A Cuban proverb reinforces this point, *"When the sun rises, it rises for everyone."* Research, meditation, decision and action are the keys to success. Dr. Viktor Frankl, the Austrian psychiatrist who survived the Nazi death camps, saw a lot before he said, *"Everything can be taken from a man but one thing: to choose one's own way."* You can choose to master success.

Dr. Viktor Frankl

THE MASTER'S CIRCLE

Enter the master's circle of studying, practicing and teaching. Mastery is not a peak to be reached but a plateau to be walked. The true master does not sit on her laurels waiting for others to pay homage but rather continues to study and practice and teach. Studying, practicing and teaching are the master's calling. This can be you. Start studying. Start practicing. Start teaching others, perhaps formally, perhaps informally but certainly through your example. Make that choice right now and enjoy forever a passionate purposeful life filled with peace and prosperity.

Study pastry baking, on-line trading, portrait painting, home building, family counseling, fashion designing, muscle building, plotting the stars, sailing your charter boat or anything else that excites you. Become the master: study, practice and teach. The master is content and smiles because she is doing what she wants to do. She is improving herself and helping others. Right now and forever.

So start now. Make a promise to yourself to read this book through to the end. Carry this book with you until you've finished it whether that's fourteen hours or fourteen days. Put it in your pack, purse or briefcase. Think about the ideas and principles as you map a glorious life for yourself. It is and always was and always will be your choice. Only 10% of Americans read one book a year. Fewer read for self-improvement. A small fraction act. Make yourself part of this elite group of book readers and forever reap the benefits. How have others succeeded? Self-education through reading is an excellent start. Two thousand years ago, the Roman statesman Seneca said, *"As long as you live, keep learning how to live."* These words survived through two millennia for a very simple reason. They represent the simple truth.

Power comes in the moment of decision. In this moment, make that decision. Decide that your life is too important to leave to chance. Decide that you want to be the best you that you can be. Right this instant make the switch from passivity to power.

KEY CONCEPTS

Simple changes in the way you think can often make the difference between personal fulfillment and misery. You possess the God given power of free will to choose the course your life will take. Think for yourself and don't permit others to stereotype you and prejudge your potential for success. Your path to success will be directed by a lifelong commitment to self-reliance and self-education. You can become a master of success by studying, practicing and teaching as you improve yourself and help others. Don't envy those who have had it easy. Take pride in your willingness to work hard. You can choose to make the next years your best years. Use the Action Principles as your guide.

YOUR ASSIGNMENT

You have already taken that first step by starting to read this book. And now we would like you to take a second step. Think about all the people you know. From this group who is the one who has shown the most desire to achieve more in life? Who among them do you have the closest rapport with? Who is the one you can always count on when the going gets tough?

This is a judgment call. A person you can trust and who will stick by you is preferable to a very ambitious but distant acquaintance. You need to call that person and tell them that in 14 days you want to meet with them for several hours to discuss something important. In 14 days you will be ready for the meeting. If he or she asks what it is about just tell them you have something important to discuss. You will need the full 14 days to prepare so don't schedule the meeting any sooner. Also, to keep your ideas fresh and your enthusiasm high, try not to go beyond 20 days after the calling date. Now is the time to call. If it is too late to call send him or her an email. If there isn't email leave a message on the answering machine.

If you made the phone call then you know just some of what it feels like to act decisively. As you made the call you felt excitement because you knew that this was something out of the ordinary. That is just a small preview of the excitement and energy you will feel in the next two weeks as you feel your personal power build.

Chapter Two
Master Goals

There is no upper limit to what individuals are capable of doing with their minds. There is no age limit that bars them from beginning. There is no obstacle that cannot be overcome if they persist and believe.
H. G. Wells, English novelist & historian (b. 1866)

Congratulations! By making that appointment you have begun your journey in the Master Success System. By taking the first step, you have already distinguished yourself as a person of action who is capable of taking control to improve your own life. This first achievement has given you a key that you will be able to use for the rest of your life.

Did you make that phone call? If not, then go back to chapter one, read the instructions, and do it. This book is not just a collection of ideas that can be simply read. It is part of a system that will only work if you follow the ideas with the necessary actions. Go ahead, change your life now by becoming a person of action. You possess the power to change. Begin right now!

This is your life. We are all like the sculptor's stone and resistant to change. You are the sculptor. You must chip away at what you don't like. Only you can pick up that hammer and chisel and do it. Only you can reach that best you that lies within the stone. Start chipping. Start making the right choices for yourself.

Beware The Naysayers

Stop asking the wrong people if you can be a professional musician or a priest or a graphic designer or a restaurant owner or a social worker. They may tell you, *"No."* They may give you every excuse in the book. They may give you every reason for failure. They may gladly recite for you the downside of any decision you could make. It will be very easy for you to rationalize and take comfort in their answers. Perhaps, they haven't succeeded, so why should you? Mark Twain saw this happening one hundred years ago when he said, *"Keep away from people who try to belittle your ambitions. Small people always do that, but the really great make you feel that you, too, can become great."*

This is not about your mother, father, spouse, partner, sister, brother, neighbor, co-worker, friend or anyone else. The well-

meaning advice of others can only serve as a catalyst for you to make your own decisions. It is about what you want and what you are willing to do to get what you want. The author Robert Louis Stevenson is quoted as saying, *"To know what you prefer instead of humbly saying Amen to what the world tells you that you ought to prefer, is to have kept your soul alive."*

Robert Louis Stevenson

Professor Leo Buscaglia shared the same sentiments when he said, *"The easiest thing to be in the world is you. The most difficult thing to be is what other people want you to be. Don't let them put you in that position."* Have you got

what it takes? Will you persevere when the going gets a little tough? Are you going to whine, whimper, complain and feel sorry for yourself when you see a few obstacles? Will you give up and settle for less than your best? Don't worry; you can never overachieve because you have unlimited potential.

Leo Buscaglia

You don't expect success to come easily. It's not easy that you're after. You simply want the chance to prove all that you can do. You'll do the work necessary to turn possibility to probability. You will feel inspired and passionate. Your life will have purpose. Two hundred years ago, the American novelist Washington Irving wrote, *"Great minds have purposes; others simply have wishes."* You will feel happy and full of joy as a missionary fulfilling your God-given potential. Stop daydreaming. Stop being lazy. Stop looking for the easy way. Stop looking for excuses. The American statesman Benjamin Franklin said, *"He that is good for making excuses is seldom good for anything else."* Stop comparing yourself to less ambitious people around you. Stop asking if you can do it and start doing it. Live with a can-do spirit. You can own the best landscaping business in town. You can be a successful lawyer. You can be a poet. You can run the marathon. You can earn an MBA. You can be a black belt. Read. Research. Join. Network. Volunteer. Intern.

ACTION IS THE KEY

You learn. You try. You make mistakes. The famous American psychologist B. F. Skinner wrote, *"A failure is not always a mistake. It may simply be the best one can do under the circumstances. The real mistake is to stop trying."* You learn. You try again. Never stop improving. Action. This is you! You have seen what others have done and are doing. What is it that you want to do? You know it can be done. Do it. Everything passes from old hands to young. There will always be new authors, new actors, new millionaires, new entrepreneurs, new politicians and new saints. Who is singing the new songs? Who owns the big buildings? Who is serving in Congress? Who is the president of the company? Who is the general? Who is setting the moral example for others to follow? Everything is changing. Be a part of the change.

B. F. Skinner

What do you want from your life? How will you define personal success? Put into writing your goals and plans. Go to your Action Principles for inspiration. Also, consider the following list of characteristics which define the style and attitudes of most successful people.

CHARACTERISTICS OF SUCCESSFUL PEOPLE

1. You have goals. You have a clear vision of who you are and where you are going. You are devoted to your own self-improvement. You aren't content just to react to life. You are result and not praise oriented. You realize that to move forward you must be committed to change. People begin to see you as a serious, purposeful person.

2. You prioritize. You figure out what are the most productive things to do and you do them. You do them even if they are difficult. You are results oriented. You are an effective time manager. You seek balance among body, mind and spirit. You don't automatically say *"Yes"* to everyone and everything.

3. You are self-reliant. Your self-image is one of confidence

25

based on capability. You believe in your abilities. You know that the overwhelming number of problems have solutions. You are a person of conviction. You don't look for others to do your work for you. You know that you are better off challenging yourself rather than competing with others. You are motivated. You are passionate about your glorious future. You are a self-starter. You are prepared to endure. You aren't paralyzed by a fear of criticism, rejection or failure. You aren't afraid to promote your own interests.

4. You are understanding and tolerant. You work to remove hate, anger, impatience, selfishness, ignorance, laziness, envy, vindictiveness and negative thinking from your life. You work to free yourself of personal prejudices. You respect the rights of others. You realize that every fight isn't your fight. You can't waste your time thinking that you are better than others. You are quick to forget the mistakes and omissions of others. You work to promote and build bridges of understanding.

5. You are tough. You face challenges. By accepting and working through these challenges, you become ever stronger. You don't give in to pressure. You don't pretend that everything is great when it isn't. As you learn and build, you aren't afraid to look foolish. You don't lie to yourself or anyone else. You are prepared to do the work and make the sacrifices necessary to get a good education, to make enough money, to get and stay fit, to be a responsible child or parent and to lead a spiritual life. Your commitment to a high moral code is apparent. You aren't looking for excuses. The odds don't frighten you. You aren't afraid of arguments that are counter to your own. You are accustomed to doing jobs that others won't. When necessary, you can exercise reason, patience and restraint. You accept that life can be unfair. You have doubts, apprehensions and fears but you proceed anyway.

6. You set the example. Your children and employees don't have to wonder how to act; they only have to watch you. You are willing to take the lead and become a role model. Your word means something. You don't seek perfection. You seek to do your personal best. You walk the talk. You take responsibility. You are diligent, consistent and dependable. You show persistence. You finish what you start. You become a luminary attracting and guiding others. Your positive example gives you influence and power to do good.

7. You maintain a positive mental attitude. You know that you will have a great future because you will create it. You take pride in the small changes that you know will eventually lead to significant achievements. You realistically accept life's annoyances and problems but you choose to deal with them with a positive, solution-oriented mindset. You control your attitude. You listen to your conscience. You know that there are no guarantees but you proceed anyway. Your life means what you say it means. You enjoy and learn from motivational books, tapes and videos. You trust yourself. You don't allow your doubts to destroy your dreams. You like the challenge of improving yourself and learning new things. You greet each new day energized.

8. You use affirmations. You stay motivated by motivating yourself. You adopt the positive habit of repeating affirmations. You write positive statements on cards and repeat them. You choose only those affirmations in which you deeply believe. Do it now. Copy success. Constantly improve. Help others. Who dares wins. Avoid pain and seek happiness. Invest today for tomorrow. Have the attitude of gratitude. You can become all that you are willing to affirm.

"Of course I hope to find gold. But my real goal is spiritual growth and inner peace."

9. You submit to a higher power. You build your life upon your faith. You cherish your faith. You aren't afraid to tell others of your beliefs. You stand for positive values. You are ethical in your dealings. You pray and meditate to have the courage to face your fears. You pray and meditate to have the strength to accept, endure and triumph over the hardships that the path to success will present. You cultivate the good that you find in the world.

10. You want to help others. You see the best in yourself and in others. You instill confidence. You want to help others achieve their goals. You reject self-centeredness. You don't wait for someone else to help. You take action. Start the ball rolling; lead and others may follow. You work hard to foster positive alliances. You accept that those people most in need of your help may be least able to thank you.

11. You seek the support of others. As you help others, you aren't too proud to ask for help yourself. As strong as you are individually, you realize that you aren't alone. Being a loving person, many people will love you. Being an inquisitive person, many people will want to help you. Being a nice person, many people will want to work for you and be your friend. Being a religious person, you have your faith in God.

12. You are decisive. You do it first. You don't procrastinate. You aren't complacent sitting around waiting for *"it"* to happen. Unless you take action, nothing happens. When something is wrong and it's your business, you take action to make it right. You concentrate and are focused. If you want to learn how to do something, begin. You aren't looking for people to validate all of your excuses. You review the facts. You consider your options. You are flexible, versatile and ready to adapt as needed. You choose the best option and you don't look back. You have self-confidence. You do what must be done. You are bold. You accept the risks of change. You don't look for excuses or to place blame. You are forthright and give it to them straight.

13. You are imitative. You look for positive role models to emulate. These are people who exhibit the character traits that you admire such as being: honest, calm, brave, friendly, generous, fair, funny, charming, forgiving, patient, intelligent, enthusiastic and competent.

14. You are inquisitive. You can learn anything that you want to learn. You seek advice. You listen. You are interested in many aspects of life and you want to learn more. You keep an open mind. Life becomes a wonderful discovery. You are open-minded and see new opportunities as new chances to learn. It would take a long time before you'd want to say that something is impossible to do. Classes, courses, seminars, speeches, websites, books, videos, audiocassettes and magazines all present opportunities for you to learn. You understand that the smart can defeat the strong. Keep questioning. You do not fear the truth. You aren't afraid to say, *"I don't know."*

15. You admit your fears and weaknesses. No one is perfect and no one is truly fearless. You are capable of being self-critical. You are teachable. When you can honestly admit your shortcomings to yourself, you are at least half the way to controlling or compensating for them. You face your fears and, in doing so, you build your character. You know that to lead a full life you must take some risks. You aren't afraid to say, *"I'm sorry. I was wrong."*

16. You learn from your mistakes. You know that the difference between successful people and others is not whether you make mistakes but how you respond to them. You know that never making a mistake is a mistake. You don't sulk because things didn't go your way. You figure out what happened and what you could have done differently. You develop new strategies. You write a new plan and you try again. When you find a better way to do something, you do it. You remember past victories. You know that mistakes are not permanent. You rise above your mistakes.

17. You seek high standards. You find your personal best and work to this level. You pride yourself on your integrity, honesty and love of justice. You appreciate that lying only leads to more lying. Everyone who meets and deals with you benefits from your commitment to being your best. You do not waiver from your principles and core values.

18. You are nice to be around. You like people. You are patient and listen. You smile. You are gentle and sympathetic. You are open to reasonable compromise. You are supportive and dependable. You respect others. You are not imposing. You compliment good work and effort. You have a good sense of humor. You are congenial, gracious, outgoing, polite and well mannered. You express gratitude for nice things done for you. You help without question or complaint. You wish others well. What goes around, comes around. You are passionate and exciting. You are cheerful and happy.

HERE IS A GLIMPSE AT YOUR REWARD

People smile as you enter a room because they are glad to see you. Your presence is always welcomed. People treat you with respect and seek your advice and approval. These people are your loving spouse, your well-behaved children, your trustworthy friends, your loyal employees and your satisfied customers.

How different are you when you follow the Action Principles? You smile, listen, call, share, volunteer, write and e-mail. You are kind, generous, modest, truthful, and courteous. When others tell of their accomplishments, you listen and applaud their efforts. You don't try to top their stories with your stories. From these simple daily actions emanate the power to live your life being needed, being wanted and making a difference. Small efforts placed well and placed often reap large rewards. If you want charisma, this is charisma. Your unselfish self-assurance will make you the frequent center of positive attention. For yourself, you are beginning to find a personal contentment in which you want less for yourself and more for others.

GOALS ARE YOUR MAP

Think about the next few years but also think long term. Where will you be in twenty years? Go further; think of yourself in old age. You'll want to be content with the best effort that you put forth. You'll want your golden years to be filled with fond memories and not with deep regrets. Plan for this to happen!

Don't let statistics get you down. Make the numbers work for you. Let's say that you would love to start your own business but you've heard repeatedly that most small businesses fail.

Henry Ford

That's true. But what you don't hear so often is that most of those failures are first time efforts. Henry Ford taught his workers, *"Failure is the opportunity to begin again more intelligently."* Second business attempts succeed far more often. The first time you're a rookie. The second time you're an experienced, battle hardened veteran. If you keep trying and keep learning, you put the odds for success in your favor.

Most people don't find it easy to move beyond life's setbacks, big or small. They get a little bruised and they rush to unburden themselves on a sympathetic audience. Of course, the selected audience is very likely to be empathetic and justify the decision to stop or quit. Any excuse can be offered except personal responsibility. That is how too many people react when their days, their years, their lives don't go their way. It should not be how you react. You are self-reliant. You are tough. Consider the words of the 17th century French moralist

Francois de la Rochefoucauld, *"Nothing is impossible; there are ways that lead to everything, and if we had sufficient will we should always have sufficient means. It is often merely for an excuse that we say things are impossible."*

Athletics teach this lesson. You are on a team and you lose a game. You may feel bad but you can't dwell on your unhappiness because you may have another game in a few days. You have to put the past away and get ready to do your best in the next game. Championship teams function with this perspective. On the journey, as you risk, dare and challenge, you will make mistakes and you may even lose a battle or two. You won't wallow in self-pity. You won't look for the nearest shoulder to cry on. You will accept the disappointment. What happened? What can you do differently the next time? Try again. You really only fail when you say that you have failed. It's only over when you quit.

A screenwriter once said that at any given time there are thousands of unsold scripts circulating around Hollywood. Your odds of success having your one script being accepted aren't very good. However, your odds for success skyrocket if you just write a second script.

Here's the reason. It is very hard to sell a script if you don't have an agent representing you and agents don't want to represent you if you are a one shot wonder. However, if you show up with two, three or four scripts and they are well written you have a good chance of getting an agent and then getting your scripts read and sold.

What both these examples show is that the things you often hear about starting a business or selling a script or other things present a distorted picture. And the picture is distorted by the fact that most people are not persistent. They try starting one business and when it doesn't immediately succeed, they never try again. Or they write just one script and then when they can't sign on with an agent they end up giving up. Too many people quit on their dreams too soon. This will not be you. You will persist. President Calvin Coolidge believed this, *"Nothing in the world can take the place of persistence. Talent will not; nothing is more common than unsuccessful men with talent. Genius will not; unrewarded genius is almost a proverb. Education will not; the world is full of educated dere-*

Calvin Coolidge

licts. Persistence and determination are omnipotent. The slogan 'press on' has solved and always will solve the problems of the human race."

BE PERSISTENT

Persistence will put you in with some pretty good company.

Before becoming president, Abe Lincoln failed at two businesses and lost six elections.

1000 banks turned down Walt Disney when he was trying to finance Disneyland.

Mary Kay Ash, a billionaire, sold less than $2.00 worth of cosmetics at her first beauty show.

Michael Jordan was cut from his high school basketball team.

Bill McGowan fought the AT&T monopoly for ten years before making MCI successful.

Mark Victor Hansen and Jack Canfield were rejected 32 times before finding a publisher for *Chicken Soup For The Soul.*

Sylvester Stallone was turned down time and time again when he was trying to produce Rocky. He couldn't even get an extra's acting job in The Godfather.

Louisa May Alcott, who wrote *Little Women,* was told by an editor that she had no talent or chance at a writing career.

Before his first job in the band Menudo, Ricky Martin, the Latin superstar, was rejected several times as being too small and young looking.

Start right now, today, to live a pro-active life – a life that you control. As soon as you set your goals and begin to take action, you are on the road and the journey has begun. Success is the journey. The easiest thing in the world and the hardest thing in the world is to change yourself. Only you can change you and you can only change you. You must have the courage to be honest with yourself. What is it going to take for you to become the best you? St. Francis De Sales instructed us, *"Do not wish to be anything but what you are, and try to be that perfectly."* No two people are going to have exactly the same list of goals and plans. One person may be physically fit but lazy at work. Someone may be a great earner but a poor investor. Another person may be the nicest person to everyone all day except when he gets home to his own family.

Look at the following life categories and decide what goals

and plans fit where you are now in your life and in what direction you'd like your journey to take.

Spiritual Goals. Spiritual goals give you an opportunity to look at the big picture. What is your relationship with God? What is your responsibility to the environment and to your fellow man? What do you intend to leave as your legacy? How will your one life have made a difference to humanity?

Family Goals. Family goals allow you to share and to enjoy life with a kindred partner and to pass on all your best qualities to a new generation. How can you be a better husband, wife, parent, aunt or uncle? Can you write a note or e-mail, call or visit a lonely family member?

Physical Goals. Physical goals challenge you to be as fit and healthy as possible. You can't change genetics or avoid all accidents but you don't have to waddle through life either. Are you exercising, watching your weight and getting enough sleep? Are you meditating or using quiet time to reduce stress and align your priorities? Have you chosen a life sport?

Career Goals. Career goals place you in a position to earn enough money to have all the material possessions and time that you want for yourself and your family. Will you work a second job or accept overtime? Will you go back to school to improve your job skills? Will you be such a valuable employee that your company will fear losing you? Will you start your own business?

Cultural Goals. Cultural goals are your opportunity to fill your life with beauty. Are you going to the theater and concerts and gallery shows? Are you savoring fine food and wines? Are you reading great books and listening to great music? Who or what is stopping you from living well?

Community Goals. Community service goals present the

chance for you to give back. Can you volunteer to work for local worthwhile causes? Can you donate money? Would you run in a race to raise money for those in need? Would you run for political office?

Social Goals. Social goals are a two way street. Do you appreciate friendships? Do you entertain? Do you offer counsel and comfort? Do you make people feel welcome? Are you neat, clean, well mannered and polite?

Intellectual Goals. Intellectual goals encourage you to commit to a life of curiosity and self-education. Books, magazines, talks, speeches, seminars, courses and the entire world of the Internet are your resources. This new millennium presents opportunities for unparalleled academic advancement. What will you do? What are your ideas for better people, families, relationships, and societies? How will you tell the world?

Investment Goals. Investment goals demand that you sacrifice today for tomorrow. Are you preparing for a long retirement? Have you taken the time to understand the benefits of your pension and other retirement plan? In what industries do you have specialized knowledge that you can put to profitable investment use? Do you know successful market investors whose advice and strategies you can copy? Would you invest in rental real estate? Do you need life or disability insurance?

Personal Goals. Personal goals – For this category, let's really expand your thinking. Make a wish without worrying about your abilities, experiences or assets. What would you be able to do? How much money would you have? What would you create? Where would you live? What sort of home would you have? Is it a mansion? A house in the country? Where would you like to visit? Would you like to tour Europe? Visit Japan? Go to Disneyland? What sort of hobbies would you enjoy if you could do whatever you liked? Would you own a pet or a luxury car? What would you do for your friends and your family? Go ahead and free your thinking.

Let your goals reflect the outcomes that you desire. What are the results and consequences of the goals you choose? You must be sure that once you attain a goal, you get exactly the outcome you had expected. After spending a year's salary on a car or seven years' salary on a house or four years earning a college degree, you don't want to feel disappointed.

CREATE YOUR MAP

On your Master Success journey, goals will serve as your map references. When you decide on the changes you want to make in your life and begin to define your goals, write them down. Many successful people regard this as a critical step. If you write it down, you are taking that first small step toward accomplishing it. It may seem to be a little thing, quite inconsequential in the grand scheme. It isn't. Taking small steps, taking action, is what really separates those who will achieve their wishes from those whose lives will just be wishful thinking. You will feel a sense of power coming from just this small bit of action. Only 3% of people have written goals. Only 1% of people review those written goals each day.

Think. Visualize. Write it down. Think again. Refine your thoughts. The strategies for appropriate action will begin to formulate in your mind. Your vision evolves into goals that become objectives, which become daily to-dos. As you write, think and act, a wonderful thing will begin to happen; it is called momentum. You will feel exhilarated. Your enthusiasm and pride in your accomplishments will spur you forward to accomplish ever more. Momentum builds. Momentum will serve to further bolster your self-confidence. In the course of researching your goals, new and better ideas will appear that will stimulate your thinking. You will constantly be customizing and refining your goal setting. These are your goals and no one else's. You may start out wanting to be a general graphic designer and then decide to specialize in web design. You may start with one diet and switch to another. You may like Tudor houses until you see Colonials. You may start as a paralegal and finish as an attorney. You begin college as a psychology major and finish with a teaching degree. These changes are for the good. Keep perfecting your personal vision of yourself, your style, your attitudes and your lifestyle.

BE BOLD AND BEGIN

What can you start to do right now from your goals' list? If you want to read more, get a book and start reading. If you want to exercise, walk around the block. If you want to be more extroverted, say hello to five people and compliment three people. If you want to do some good, visit with a lonely person

Susan B. Anthony

in a nursing home, hospital, shelter or prison. Get going. It will be hard. It will seem new and awkward. You may fall back as you move ahead. Get going. These small accomplishments will embolden you to do more and more. You are a person of action. Listen to the great American feminist Susan B. Anthony. *"Cautious, careful people, always casting about to preserve their reputations ... can never effect a reform."* This is the journey. This is your journey.

Let's say you want to get rich in real estate and retire in twenty years. Go to the library and read every book they have on real estate. This is but the start of a lifelong self-education process. Get a real estate license. Start talking to landlords and real estate agents. Start reading the classified ads. If you have no money to invest, that is your problem to solve. Start working part-time as a rental agent. Get a second night job at the mall. Join the National Guard. Find a partner. Do what you have to do to acquire the funds you'll need to become an investor. There is a way. Find it. Go to the bookstore for more books. Search on-line and keep reading. Take the Master Real Estate course on MasterSuccess.com. Commit to your success. List all the people who can help you to realize your goals: lawyer, accountant, business associates, employees, friends, family members, investment advisors, bankers, teachers, counselors, neighbors, mentors, club members. Start a contact-networking file. Make a list of people to whom you can delegate tasks or whom you can hire to work with you toward the accomplishment of your goals.

If you are committed to the Action Principles, who or what can stop you? There are no excuses. The Nobel Laureate Dr. Albert Schweitzer reminds us, *"One who gains strength by overcoming obstacles possesses the only strength which can overcome adversity."* If you are starting with absolutely nothing, you will simply savor your success that much more. Prove your critics wrong. Play to your strengths. You write the rules. You do what you have to do. Do it for yourself and for those you love. Take out that pencil and paper or go to your computer and start now. Map your life.

Dr. Albert Schweitzer

Goals are your life's blueprint. If you were asked, you should be able to recite your major goals. Let no one doubt your determination to succeed. You will be so excited and motivated by your goals that you can't take no for an answer.

LET YOUR IDEAS FLOW

Perhaps you'd like to make a list of 100 things that you'd like to do in your life. Visit Paris. Run the marathon. Start a business. Own a red sports car. Golf with a 10 handicap. Put your children through college. Each day, choose an Action Principle for reflection. Are you getting any useful ideas for adding new goals or redefining established goals?

If you could change lives with someone else, who would it be?

What goals would you attempt if you had no fear?

What projects have you started but haven't finished?

What do you feel you were born to do?

What is missing from your life?

Goal setting gives you control over the direction of your life's journey. Goal setting is personal power. Many, through inaction, will rest their futures on the hard work or benevolence of others. You have one life. Why risk that life on another's whim or another's plan for you? Set goals and assume control of your own life. The goals you select should be challenging but realistic and achievable. Goals that are too easy or too hard can negatively affect your motivation.

Since the Master Success journey is ongoing, so goal setting is ongoing. Commitment to a life of ongoing self-improvement and service to others takes you from one goal to the next. An interest in government in high school may lead to a major in political science in college to earning a law degree to a successful career as an attorney to a judgeship to semi-retirement as legal aid advocate. Goals become the markers from one point to another. Be great. Believe. Go for it. Hear the words of Ralph Waldo Emerson, *"Nothing great has ever been accomplished without enthusiasm."*

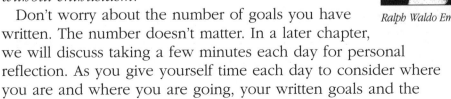

Ralph Waldo Emerson

Don't worry about the number of goals you have written. The number doesn't matter. In a later chapter, we will discuss taking a few minutes each day for personal reflection. As you give yourself time each day to consider where you are and where you are going, your written goals and the

Carl Sandburg

corresponding plans for achieving those goals will naturally evolve from one to the next. You will be amazed at how inspired and confident you feel about your journey. You will be focused. Your goals will be clarified and focused. Let Lincoln scholar Carl Sandburg be your guide, *"The time for action is now. It's never too late to do something."*

KEY CONCEPTS

Successful people have left a clear example of attitudes and actions for you to follow. The success you achieve will be from your own initiative. You don't look for others to do your work for you. You know you must be tough enough to face challenges. You are prepared to do the work and make the sacrifices necessary to achieve your goals. You will be an example to others.

You maintain a positive mental attitude by approaching problems with an action-oriented mindset. You use positive affirmations to keep your mind on track. You seek out positive inspirational books, tapes and videos. You associate with positive people. You look for positive role models and copy success. You help others achieve their goals.

You must be decisive. You don't want to wait for things to happen. You need to go out and make them happen by choosing the best option and committing to it fully. To be decisive you must accept risk and move forward.

When setting goals you need to think long term. You need to make decisions, set priorities. No two people will have the same set of goals. You must examine every area of your life and decide what it is that you wish to achieve. You must be prepared to be persistent. You should start today and then continue every day for the rest of your life. You want to be one of the 1% of people who have written goals and review them every day.

YOUR ASSIGNMENT

Your next assignment is to write a one-page personal mission statement. If you haven't read through all of the Action Principles at least once, do that now. Writing a Mission Statement is one of the Action Principles. Also, review the success characteristics outlined earlier in this chapter. Your mission statement should be specific about what you want and what you are going to do to get it. It should be stated positively – 'I will be wealthy' not 'I won't be poor.' It is best to define what you mean by wealthy. Do you mean $100,000 or $1,000,000? The more specific the better. Include one or two sentences from each of your goal categories.

You are describing yourself at your best. Read your personal mission statement each morning when you get up and in the evening before you go to sleep. This should feel liberating and exciting. You have now created a map for your own life. This is a defining moment. This will be a day to remember.

You are well on your way.

CHAPTER THREE
MASTER TIME

*Everything requires time. It is the only truly universal condition.
All work takes place in time and uses up time. Yet most people
take for granted this unique irreplaceable and necessary
resource. Nothing else, perhaps, distinguishes effective
executives as much as their tender loving care of time.*
Peter Drucker, Management consultant (b. 1909)

Time is your life. Therefore, becoming a master of time is
essential. If you haven't read through the Action Principles or
written your mission statement; today is the day; now is the
moment. If you're headed in the wrong direction, it doesn't matter how fast you're going. There is a German proverb that says,
"What's the use of running if you're not on the right road?" You
need a map and your written mission statement and goals are
that map. Time is not a renewable resource. God has given us
time and the free will to use it. You do not want to squander
this precious gift. This is your one life. You repay God by
becoming an effective time manager and leading an
exemplary life.

Mastering time is choosing to live your life consciously and aware of what you're doing and why
you are doing it. Leo Tolstoy, the Russian novelist,
wrote, *"There is only one time that is important –
NOW! It is the most important time because it is the
only time that we have any power."* You don't want to

Leo Tolstoy

fall into a tedious daily routine where the mundane
activities of one day simply lead to the mundane
activities of the next day. This isn't living. This is existing.

START ORGANIZING

Each day you'll need to write a prioritized to-do list. Some people like to keep it simple and jot down three to five priorities for the day on an index card. The back of the card is used for appointments and phone calls. Most computers come with a built-in personal organizer and scheduling programs for those who prefer to work from a more detailed and extensive daily plan. The important point is not the planning format but the fact that you have a written prioritized to-do list to guide you through each day. Each day becomes significant and each day brings you one day closer to realizing your goals.

Save your daily to-do lists for annual review. It's educational and motivational to see the incremental steps that you have taken to reach your objectives. In addition, this analysis will serve as a valuable reference when you undertake the master's job of mentoring and teaching.

A BORING LIFE IS YOUR FAULT

If you lead a boring life, this is your personal problem. To live a full life, you must accept the promise and risks of change. Often, you must move outside your comfort zone. Life is not standing still waiting for you.

Some people waste hours.

Some people waste their entire lives.

If it's your fun time, you should be having fun and not worrying about your investments. Be in the moment. If it's your quiet time, be quiet. Live your life on purpose and your goals and planning will give you that purpose. When you choose to live your life on purpose, you will be putting your time to its best use. You can't always choose what happens to you. You can always choose how you react to what happens to you.

Initially, goal setting and planning may seem like a lot of work. So be it. This is not a step to skip or to take for granted. Start today to write daily goals and in 21 days you will have begun to form an important positive habit. In this short three weeks, goal setting and planning will begin to become second nature. You consider options. You make choices. You are decisive. You gain confidence. With confidence, you become even better at decision making. You become increasingly proficient in separating the urgent and the important from the interesting but inconsequential.

Most people don't set daily goals. Of course, most people

don't write hit songs, make a million dollars in real estate, get elected mayor, start successful businesses, retire early or raise self-reliant happy children. You can make progress every day on your success journey. Start today. To master time, you need a daily plan of action.

WRITTEN GOALS AND PLANS BACKED WITH DECISIVE ACTION ARE THE ANSWER.

Without clear goals, ambition or firm direction, the tendency will be to spend too much time doing small easy tasks, leaving insufficient time and energy for the larger, more difficult and, perhaps, more important projects. You start settling for less than what was possible. Perhaps you are even missing rewards that

were within your grasp but that you didn't see. Are some tasks worth doing at all? Which tasks are urgent and must be done immediately? What activities are time sensitive and which aren't? Which tasks are important but can be planned? You set your priorities. Your aim is not simply to do more work but to get the more important work done. Malcolm X once said, *"In all our deeds, the proper value and respect*

Malcolm X   *for time determines success or failure."*

BEWARE THE SKILLED TIME WASTERS

As one involved in the Master Success System, you will often

be called upon to assume a leadership position. Therefore as both a supervisor and an example you should be aware of the different types of time wasters that you may encounter. From the American statesman Benjamin Franklin, *"Lost time is never found again."* The Victorian English author Charles Dickens warned that *"Procrastination is the thief of time."*

Benjamin Franklin   There are do-nothing people. Do-nothing is an attitude and not a social program. Do-nothing people are not necessarily unemployed. They may be very skilled and ingenious at doing nothing. They may have found a way to blend in while *"working"* for large corporations, government or educational institutions. They may have found a nothing to-do niche or even created such a position for themselves. Many of these people have an over-inflated self-esteem and think that they are too good for the work that others suppose they are doing. They may feel under-appreciated and, as long as they can get away with it, entitled to do little or nothing while others work.

Then, there are the perfectionist types. Perfectionists may seem like hard workers, even workaholics, but while appearing busy they never accomplish very much. They will flutter and fidget endlessly on small details. They are endless information gatherers and endless planners who can't make decisions. They worry about too many things that will never happen. For perfectionists, it is safer to work on small jobs and small problems because in doing so they can only make small mistakes and thus avoid confrontation and criticism. They appear to be above average workers, students or children when they are not.

Both types of professional time wasters may talk a good game but scrutiny of their behaviors tells a truer story. They may be well dressed and carry attachés and clipboards. They look like they belong while contributing little or nothing to an organization's progress. Of course, time wasters aren't only found in work environments. They can be found anywhere. A supervisor, teacher or parent must have clear organizational goals and periodic performance reviews to identify skillful non-achievers.

In the short term, the time wasters around you may seem to be the smart ones who are beating the system, but don't envy them. The parasite has few friends. You have chosen a more difficult but honorable path. Yes, there may be an easier road but you have not chosen this road. You will be self-reliant. Be proud that you are always willing to do your share and more. You will be able to stand tall. Your conduct will be masterful.

You will never be wasting time if you are improving yourself and helping others.

COMMON TIME WASTERS

Here are a few typical time wasters to guard against:
- Not planning or poor planning
- Lack of self-discipline
- Not prioritizing tasks
- Mistakes
- Pointless meetings
- Perfectionism
- Poor communication
- Equipment failure
- Unwarranted demands by or on others
- Not listening or ignoring instructions

- Socializing during work time
- Inability to make decisions
- Lack of motivation or interest
- Inability to say *"No"*
- Inability to delegate
- Procrastination

Be a person of action. Demand excellence of yourself in all your endeavors. However, concentration on impossible standards in one area can only lead to imbalance in other areas. To find peace and happiness, you need to balance all areas of your life. If you're starving yourself to be on the high school wrestling team or to be a cheerleader, your priorities are misplaced. If you are always working nights until 10p.m. to get a promotion and are ignoring your family, any monetary benefits of the promotion aren't worth the lost family time. If your priorities are misaligned, you will be wasting time. The German poet Johann Wolfgang von Goethe said, *"Things that matter most should never be at the mercy of things that matter least."*

Johann Wolfgang von Goethe

WORK AT THE PERSONAL MASTERY LEVEL

As you commit to a life of self-improvement, it is important to differentiate your path from the slippery slope of perfectionism. Man is human and therefore can never become a perfect master.

Your pursuit of the best you is an ideal pursuit. Your pursuit of perfection would be an unhappy endless obsession. You want to work at a high level in all your endeavors as you continually improve toward your personal best. This journey is personal mastery.

For a student, a grade of 90 is attainable and laudable. When a student is pressured to do any more, the student may become fixed on the testing rather than the learning. If you get a 90, pat yourself on the back, relax and do something else constructive. Next term, you can take a more challenging course. This concept of the 90% level can be applied to many areas of your life. If your car and house are 90% of what you would wish, relax and re-evaluate. If your sales performance is better than 90% of your colleagues, relax and re-evaluate. Learn to relax and re-evaluate at the 90% level, the *"A"* level, of whatever you're doing and you'll be much happier and, in the long run, a much better user of time.

By committing to personal mastery, you will win many races

without having to feel inadequate when you don't win all the races. While you will wish to allot time in your schedule for professional development, you don't have to go to an Ivy League college, become the company president, drive an expensive car or live in a huge house to be successful. Spending your time acquiring grander and grander possessions is a hopeless trap. The guy with the big boat is probably spending most of his time working on the big boat. Work to your own personal master level and relax. When you have a nice house, a vacation property, one or two nice cars and reasonable savings for emergencies and retirement, you are a winner. You have won the financial game. Now, concentrate on your hobbies, family and doing good for others. This is mastering time. If you want to work harder at work and earn much more, make sure that it's for a very good reason such as early retirement.

BENEFITS OF TIME MANAGEMENT

If you are organizing your days by means of a written daily to-do list and reading your mission statement every day, you are one in a hundred. Be proud of yourself for making this important choice.

To understand how to master time, continue to examine how productively you are spending your time. For example, if you are an average American adult, you now spend four hours per night watching television. Is this the life you want? Can you plan your television viewing so that you are watching only the programs that you really want to watch? Now, we have the Internet, which is a wonderful research and entertainment medium but also a seductive consumer of your time.

How would your personal relationships, your family and society benefit from your having extra time?

Don't get into the bad habit of giving up your sleep time. You will find some people who claim to get only 3-5 hours of sleep per night. However, watching infomercials at 4a.m. and then spending the day walking around in a semi-brain fog and being grouchy are not conducive to successful living. Sleeping is restorative. For the majority of people, getting less than 7-8 hours of sleep is not a time management skill to develop. Sleep deprivation can make you cranky, weak, sick and old before your time.

TIME WASTING IS A CHOICE

Many people do not plan because they don't want change. They don't want to make choices and yet avoidance is a choice and often a poor one. They don't want to start anything that holds the possibility for disappointment, disapproval or failure. Again, some are lazy. Others will engage in mindless, time wasting activities to avoid dealing with serious life situations like bad relationships, disruptive children, or money and personal emotional problems. In the latter category are those pretend do-gooders who involve themselves in everyone else's problems to avoid dealing with their own. They can justify letting their own lives pass while they move from someone else's crisis to someone else's crisis.

You are not spending your time wisely if you are out saving the world while abdicating your own responsibilities at home.

Once you master time you will be different. What will you do with all this extra time? Improve yourself and help others? Giving of your time is a precious gift. Start with those closest to you.

You will not only take action, but you will take the right action. As you plan and organize and choose, keep these words of Dr. Martin Luther King with you, *"The time is always right to do what is right."*

Dr. Martin Luther King

USING AN ACTIVITY LOG

Many time management systems advocate the use of an activity log. Over the course of a week, you record each activity throughout the day. Are you working, eating, sleeping, primping, planning, traveling, or gossiping? Your hope in keeping the log is to identify non-productive patterns of behavior that you can alter. Don't kid yourself. It is clear that most people don't need a log to tell themselves ways to improve. Most are painfully aware of what changes they should be making.

They just have to commit to those changes and they have to be persistent for the 21 days that it takes to replace an old, bad habit with a new, good habit. In the first century, Ovid, the Roman poet, wrote, *"Habits change into character."*

For example, reading business books is a positive activity. If you can't find enough time to read, you

Ovid

can buy books on tape and listen to the tapes during morning drive time. This is a choice. If you don't pay bills until you have four copies of each bill, you will be deluged with paperwork. Make the choice to pay bills on the day they arrive. Handle paper once. Take charge of your desktop. Clean your desktop before you leave each night. If you take an hour for lunch and just gab, take a half-hour and gab. Be aware of how you are spending your time so that you can make the best choices for yourself.

GETTING ORGANIZED

There is an old Persian proverb which says, *"Luck is infatuated with the efficient."* Get organized. People respect organization. Being organized, you will find yourself with less stress and with more room, time and money. The heart of organization goes right back to goal setting and planning. Know what you want. Prioritize. Guard your work time. Eliminate interruptions. Get the job done with a positive mental attitude and don't get distracted arguing or socializing.

Put a price on your time and interests. Spend your time doing what you want to do. What smaller jobs can you have others do so that you can concentrate on higher priority tasks? You may find that hiring others to do ordinary tasks for you is not an expense but a cost-effective investment. If you hate housekeeping, hire a cleaning service. If you don't like mowing the lawn, hire a landscaping company. In most areas, you can find a host of service providers from dog walkers to handymen to grocery delivery services to nannies to personal shoppers.

How about your job situation? If you are being constantly interrupted and getting bogged down on routine tasks, you may benefit from hiring a secretary or a personal assistant. If you are engaged in a big project, hiring temporary workers may be warranted. Hiring exceptional personnel will produce long-term dividends for you and your company. If you see a hard worker with a pleasant personality at the video store or deli or the bank or anywhere, this may be a person that you'd like to hire. Give them a copy of this book and watch them shine. Then, watch your work load decrease, productivity increase or both.

You live in a world of technological wonders. You must have a computer and probably a cell phone. Look for other equipment gadgets that can make your life and job easier. Can you make use of an electronic organizer, digital camera, fax machine or mini-voice recorder?

As an organized person you will find that you will be doing one task at a time. You will make sure that you know what to do before you start a job so that you don't waste time doing the wrong thing. Your objective is to take enough time to do things right the first time. The American poet Henry Wadsworth Longfellow wrote, *"It takes less time to do a thing right than to explain why you did it wrong."*

Henry Wadsworth Longfellow

LEARNING TO SAY NO

Are you in control of your life? Or are your parents, children, spouse, bosses, employees, friends, television or addictions? There are a lot of people, places and things vying for your time. What do you want to do or have to do? Your daily to-do list enables you to prioritize the people and activities in your life and then to invest your time accordingly.

You want to help your family and friends. You do not have to be their servant. Are some customers and clients more work than they are worth? Avoid those who are time wasters and are not bringing you closer to your goals.

Bring your schedule and calendar with you to meetings. Defend your schedule, your goals, your plans, and your to-do list. If you can avoid it, don't say, *"I'll get back to you."* This creates a future obligation and more work. If you can make a decision on the spot, do that. If you have the authority, weigh commitments to new projects carefully before agreeing to them. Be prepared when requests are made of your time and resources. Does the task fit with your priorities and skills? Will the new task interfere with your present workload? Do you understand the specific requirements of the task? Are the time and performance expectations realistic? The best time to deal with any potential problems is before you assume responsibility for the task.

Discourage people from just dropping in and interrupting your work. If you have a secretary or assistant, they can take messages and arrange appointments for you. Voice mail and e-mail have a place in protecting your work time. Be sure that you have the skills, time and resources to complete requests before accepting them and allowing them to interfere with current projects.

HOW TO DELEGATE

You get a lot done. You can accomplish more when others help. Whether you are leading your family, company or softball team, you must be able to delegate assignments. Delegating means to pass responsibility to others. Delegating helps you to concentrate on what you do best and allows you to think, plan and improve organizational efficiency. You delegate tasks that are cost and time effective for others to do for you. You also delegate tasks that people can do better than you can do.

Here are a few suggestions on effective delegating:
- Match the right person to the right task.
- Explain as precisely as possible your expectations for the task.
- Establish a date when you expect the task to be completed.
- Be sure that sufficient time and resources are available to complete the task.
- Ask the person to assume responsibility for the task.
- Encourage feedback if problems develop.
- Ensure that the person understands the task and due date.
- Schedule times and methods for checks and updates.
- Say, *"Thank you."*
- Follow up.

HOW TO MANAGE PROJECTS

As you plan, you will be translating your goals into manageable sized projects. You will do this by asking yourself a number of questions:

Exactly what has to be done?

How important is the project to you and the company?

Who is assuming responsibility for the project?

Is there a deadline? Is there a start date?

What is the estimated time for the completion of the project?

How much will it cost and do you have the resources?

Besides money, what other resources are needed and are they on hand?

How will success be measured?

What projects will be postponed to complete this project?
What are my options for completing the project?
With whom can I brainstorm?
To whom can I delegate?

KEY CONCEPTS

To master your life you must master time. Each day you must have a prioritized to-do list. Whether it is written on an index card or logged in a computer you need to plan each and every day.

Focus on the matter at hand. Be aware of the typical ways people waste time and guard against them. Put a price on your time. Spend your time doing what you want to do. When people try to convince you to do things you know aren't that important, learn to say no. Your time is your life.

You must set clear goals in order to guide you in prioritizing your daily plans. Be careful that you are not devoting all your time to the small, easy tasks while the important, more difficult projects are avoided.

Discover your own time wasting habits. Adopt new, more effective habits. Stick with these habits for 21 days and they will be a part of you. Instead of getting involved in solving other people's problems, start by improving yourself. Don't engage in activities that are nothing more than ways to avoid dealing with your own situation.

Learn to delegate. Delegating helps you to concentrate on what you do best. Delegate tasks that are more cost and time effective for others to do.

YOUR ASSIGNMENT

Your assignment for this chapter during the next 21 days is:

1. Observe people around you and identify the best time managers. What lessons can you learn from them?

2. Monitor your own activities, looking for personal patterns of time wasting that can be changed. Consider how any freed time can be put to more productive use for you, your family and society.

3. Write and follow your daily to-do list and each day read your mission statement.

CHAPTER FOUR
MASTER WORK

The average person puts only 25 percent of his energy and ability into his work. The world takes off its hat to those who put in more than 50 percent of their capacity and stands on its head for those few-and-far-between souls who devote 100 percent.
Andrew Carnegie, American industrialist (b. 1835)

Let's earn money the old fashioned way by working hard. Some people are content to take life as it comes. You are ambitious. This is a good quality. Don't be ashamed of making money. This is why you work. When you are at work you will work. You will focus on those aspects of your job which are the most productive for the company whether you are an entrepreneur working for yourself or an employee working for others. Just this, working at your job, will set you apart from much of your competition for customers or promotions. You invest both in yourself and in your company through self-training and self-education. Whatever work you choose, you will become an expert in the field. First you learn how to make enough money to pay your bills. Then you learn how to make more money than you need so that you can save. Finally you learn to invest so that other people can make money for you.

Keep it simple. Other people have the money. You want it. You need it. You need money to pay your bills, to spoil yourself and to care for those close to you. To save. To invest. To retire. To help others. How do you get people to give you their money? There are three basic choices. You work for someone else. You start your own business. You seek a middle ground by becoming a commissioned salesperson.

It won't be necessary for you to go overboard and promise to work 60, 70, or 80 hours a week. If you work 40 to 50 hours a week and actually work most of those hours with a written prioritized to-do list, you will meet your objectives.

Have a purpose and then proceed with passion.

This is your life of action. Challenge yourself to live the life you want and have the things you want to have. You don't want to go to dental school because your parents wished it. What do you want? Better to become a happy artist if you want to be an artist than to remain a depressed attorney hating the daily routine of the law. If you know what you want to do, why

Pablo Picasso

waste your life doing otherwise? If you don't know what you want to do, finding direction in your life must be a priority. The 17th century English poet Samuel Butler said, *"Every man's work, whether it is literature or music or pictures or architecture or anything else, is always a portrait of himself."* Pablo Picasso offered this insight on the relationship of life and working, *"It is in your work in life that is the ultimate seduction."*

WORKING FOR WAGES OR SALARY

For most of your life, work will take up a third or more of your days. You don't want just any boring old job. You don't want to spend all this time with co-workers who are talking sports if you want to talk opera or vice versa. You want a job that matches your interests with your talents. You want to work with compatible people. Why settle for anything less?

Getting the right job is a full-time job. Work on your own and through agencies. Spend hours researching on the Internet. Involve everyone you can in your job search and encourage them to scout for openings and contacts on your behalf. Don't be shy about asking everyone for advice and help. Send out resumes but look for more creative ways to get an interview. Research the company on the Internet before your interview. Keep calling and keep a positive attitude. If you are strongly committed to a particular field, consider part-time employment and temporary assignments. Join and network through the trade associations in your chosen field. Try to find a mentor.

If you don't like your present job, this is your problem. Don't spend months and years complaining and being miserable. The solution is to devote your nights and weekends to finding another job, where you feel happy and appreciated.

Show up for your interview on time and appropriately

dressed. Act friendly and confident. Be sure to hear the interviewer's name and use it. The company is interested in how you can help them. Have your research on the company done. Don't brag about your qualifications or your personal ambitions. Don't ask too many questions about salary and benefits. Speak in terms of your willingness to help the company achieve its objectives.

When you start working, consider your initial pay as your minimum wage. You must be consciously aware of opportunities for advancement. If you start out making $10/hour, how can you make $15/hour or $20/hour? You aren't idly passing time. You are immediately figuring out who gets raises and promotions and why. Who gets the overtime or access to the best accounts? Who makes these decisions? Some people start off as the fry cook and in ten years they are the fry cooks. Some people start off as the fry cook and in ten years they own the franchise.

Wake up. Many people are hard workers. Many others are slackers who seem to pass the workday half-asleep. Slackers aren't bad people. In fact, you love slackers because they are the ones who are creating advancement opportunities for you. Take advantage.

FRY COOK TO FRANCHISE OWNER

How do fry cooks become the franchise owners? You know. It happens because of persistence, determination, hard work, goals, etc. They have a plan. They do what is necessary to move to shift supervisor to assistant manager to manager. Add in many hours of overtime. Add in the sacrifices they make by taking over work assignments for absent employees. Add in many hours devoted to studying the fast food business. Add in extra efforts that they make to let their bosses look good. Add in five years earning a Bachelor's degree on their off time. Add in saving a lot of the little money that they are earning. Add in getting franchiser approvals and finding partners and getting bank financing. This may be a ten or twelve year plan.

It won't be easy.

Few will persevere.

But, some will.

How hard are you willing to work for yourself and those you love?

Some twenty-three-year-old is going to be a winner at thirty-five. Someone at thirty-five will be a winner at forty-seven. They will persist and win.

Let this be you!

What are your interests? What is your temperament and aptitude? What is the present condition and long range projections for in the field you wish to enter? What are your present skills and talents? What kinds of work do you find easy? What is your ideal job? Sure, computers and the Internet will make lots of new millionaires and a few billionaires. Yes, high tech jobs are great but don't forget all the low-tech opportunities that will always exist. There are 5,000 different kinds of businesses and you can make money at all of them. You can get rich picking up garbage, selling fish, painting houses, teaching Spanish, paving driveways, catering parties or just about any other product or service that you can imagine. It is all about you and your style and your attitude and your hunger to succeed.

As you search for opportunities, you also will find dead ends. You may be the fry cook and quickly surmise that management, since they can't find replacements, would be very happy keeping you forever. In this circumstance, it won't matter how hard you work because promotions and respect are being saved for others. This is unfair but the real world of business is not about fairness. Your career may be ruled by the simple fact that you are just too good at frying potatoes to be replaced. You've got to replace yourself. This is your problem to resolve.

STAY AWAKE AT WORK

When you are working for someone else, you aren't in total control. This means that you must be aware and sensitive to changes at your workplace. Are new perspectives being sought? Are new priorities being initiated? Are new alliances being formed? Are you part of the new changes or part of the old guard? Awareness is not paranoia. Awareness in a corporate environment is self-reliance and self-preservation. You are responsible for yourself. In the final analysis, whatever career path you have chosen, you are really working for yourself. You have to manage your own career watching for promotion opportunities while listening for downsizing rumors. Be a reality thinker and not a wishful thinker.

You can't be passive. You've got to develop a sense for self-preservation and self-promotion. What is happening at work? Keep your eyes and ears open. Do you work for a company that clearly isn't investing money in new ideas or technology? Do you see employee discontent and customer complaints on the rise? How important are you to the company? Are you stuck in a position where you could easily be blamed for mistakes that are beyond your control? If the company is sold or taken over, how secure is your job? If you are laid off, what are your options? Are you working for a company or in an industry that is sinking? Horseshoes, sun lamps and typewriters are almost obsolete. If you were the consumer, would you do business with your company? Are competitors' products just as good or better than yours? Maybe you should plan to get out and find another job while the getting is good. Be realistic. Your loyalty to your company may be admirable but not necessarily reciprocal.

WHEN TO FIND A NEW JOB

It may be time to look for a new job if:
- your job is boring
- your co-workers aren't compatible
- the company isn't ethical
- your hard work isn't recognized
- the boss's son and you are vying for the same job
- the company isn't investing back into the company
- the atmosphere is always in crisis mode
- top management is jumping ship
- the company can't borrow money or has borrowed too much money
- the long range outlook for your industry is poor

Conversely, perhaps you work for a company with a great spirit where everyone is committed to quality. The company is preparing for major expansion. Are you ready to climb up the responsibility ladder and, of course, to profit by buying more stock in your company?

You have to put yourself in a position to make more money than you need so that you have funds to invest. You must invest so that eventually your investments will be substantial enough that you can stop working. Realize that for many working people today, this day will never come. They will have no alternative but to keep working to support themselves. They will live in constant fear of management finding a legal loophole to get rid of them. You don't want to find yourself still at work at eighty years old mumbling to yourself all day about the mistakes you made with your life. This isn't funny. This will be the sad reality for too many.

Save yourself. Start anywhere and improve every day. If you are a lawyer, a graphic designer, an aide in a nursing home or a fry cook, commit to continuous improvement. If you are flipping burgers, you've got to get a better job. Plot your escape immediately. Or, figure out what it's going to take to gain admission to the manager-training program. Do what you're paid to do. Come up with ideas for improvement. Do something extra. Be fair to those who report to you. Make your boss look good.

If you are an accountant, you've got to study the most successful accountants and start doing what they are doing. If you're a teacher or police officer or anyone on a fixed salary, you've got to apply for overtime and learn how to move up the ranks or, get a second job or start your own part-time business.

If there are people around you who are telling you all that you can't do or shouldn't do, weigh their advice carefully. However, if your conclusion is that by following the Master

Theodore Roosevelt

Success System you can reach your goals, then go for it. Let your commitment to the Action Principles separate you from the crowd. Be brave. This is your only life. President Theodore Roosevelt lived by these words, *"Far better it is to dare mighty things, to win glorious triumphs, even though checkered by failure, than to rank with those poor spirits who neither enjoy much nor suffer much because they live in the gray twilight that knows neither victory nor defeat."*

ALL JOBS ARE NOT CREATED EQUAL

In a capitalist society, there is a wide disparity in earning potential: most engineers and investment bankers make a lot of money while most fast food workers and nursing home aides make little.

Are you in a profession where your talents and initiative translate to earnings or are your wages set? You can be a great city bus driver but if you are in a union, your salary may be identical to a city bus driver with little ambition and a poor record. Or, you could be in an airline pilots union and make a six-figure income with loads of benefits.

Do you want job security? Are you a self-starter who can work independently or do you need guidance and supervision? Are you able and willing to invest time and money to secure a better career?

There are good reasons why some jobs pay more than others. Many high paying jobs such as engineering involve an investment of years of study while you incur mountains of debt. Some, such as mining, may involve physical danger. Others like working on oil tankers or military careers demand long periods of separation from your loved ones. Commissioned sales of real estate and stocks can be very lucrative but also necessitate a strong backbone to put up with all the rejection, income fluctuation, time wasted on unproductive leads and working odd hours. Start a small business and you may make several false starts before you begin to rake in the profits.

Everything about making money comes back to the Action Principles: persistence, determination, hard work coupled with a clear view of who is going to give you their money and why.

Successful people have trained themselves to be alert to problems and opportunities. Can you correct a potential problem before it escalates into a crisis? Can you seize and take advantage of opportunity while it's hot?

Successful people aren't just going through the motions at work. They are constantly thinking and evaluating their positions. Take pride in your work. You are not at work to socialize and make friends. You are at work to work. Be aware. Are those around you primarily focused on customer service or focused on doing the minimum required to not get fired? Will some of your co-workers be resentful and jealous of your ambition? Yes, they might. If most of your co-workers spend the first half-hour of the day chatting and gossiping and drinking coffee and you get right to work, will some slackers think of you as an anti-social loner? Yes, they might. If you are following the Master Success System, you will be a valuable employee. When you are interviewed for a new job, be proud of the fact that you are a fast learner and a hard worker. You put yourself on the

James Garfield

line with these comments but if you seek advancement, you want to be challenged and you want to be noticed.

Follow the words of former American President James Garfield, *"Ambition by itself never gets anyone anywhere until it forms a partnership with hard work."*

WORKING ON COMMISSION

If you can sell, it doesn't matter if you went to a big name college, a no name school or no school. Performance counts. You can sell real estate, insurance, radio advertising, automobiles, airplanes, cosmetics, clothes, vacations or mutual funds. You can represent models, athletes, musicians, and artists. What are the sales jobs behind those products or services that you love? Join those sales forces. Make your fortune.

Salespeople rule. Every company relies on its sales force. All the jobs in the company depend on the sales force's ability to sell. A person who can bring in business is a very valuable asset. That is why sales people are highly paid professionals. Most people can't do their job. They can't work alone. They can't knock on doors. They take rejection personally.

If you have the courage to talk to customers about buying a quality product or service at a fair price, your fortune is made. Forget the advanced college degrees. You don't need partners or venture capitalists. You don't need start-up capital. You don't need your own business. You already are your own business. You are already among the business elite. If you have courage to knock on doors, offer a fair deal and follow through with service, your fortune is made. Save, invest and retire young.

If you can understand and accept the following little reality of marketing, you can be a successful commissioned salesperson. *"Some will. Some won't. So what? Next!"*

As a salesperson, you should tell everyone you meet what you do for a living. Every person is a potential customer or a lead to a potential customer. Businesscards are cheap. They are your calling cards. Hand out lots of them. A businesscard is an effective and inexpensive one-to-one marketing tool. The best salespeople can tell you convincingly in two minutes or less why you should buy their product or service.

58

How do you become a successful salesperson? You learn all you can about your product or service. You learn all you can about your customers' needs. You learn all you can about sales. And, you look for the sales leaders in your industry. Find them. Take them to breakfast or lunch. Find out what they are doing. Do what they are doing. This sounds simple. This is simple.

Where do you find mentors and superstar advisors? That's your job. Read the trade papers. Research on the web. Join all the applicable trade organizations. Above all, ask. Who is the best? Ask. Who makes the most money? Ask. How do you meet these people? Ask. If you want to go into the real estate business, would you like to have breakfast with the best salesperson in your area? Ask. Someone new asking for their advice on getting started will not intimidate most successful people. In fact, they will probably be flattered. If you listen, take their advice and later follow-up by telling them that you have acted based on their advice, you may well end up with a valuable mentor. Sell yourself. Ask. Listen. Say thank you. Follow-up.

Don't be surprised if your superstar role model is a goal-oriented person who is customer service oriented and works hard. You know this. Your role model will only confirm everything that you've learned from the Action Principles and the Master Success System.

Always remember that the key to successful commissioned sales is to offer a quality product or service at a fair price. It is your job to make sure that whatever you are selling meets these criteria. To be an effective salesperson, to be believable, you must believe in your product or service. It is your responsibility to know that your customer is getting a good deal and not simply that they are ignorant of the fact that they could get a better deal down the street or on the Internet. You want your customers to be satisfied with their purchases. You want every new customer to become a regular customer. You want

your regular customers to become your sales ambassadors singing your praises and giving you leads to new customers.

Beware of commissioned sales opportunities that sound too good to be true. They are too good to be true. Be suspicious of working in a packed sales office where all your equipment is a telephone and all your training is to read a corny script. Be equally suspicious of being invited to convention size rally type events where average people seem overly eager to give up good jobs to sell Internet or telephone services, coins, under-wear or anything else. You can't make a thousand dollars a week at home stuffing envelopes. Setting up house parties to sell merchandise is tough work and you'll run out of friends fast. You won't be in business for the long term if your real business is to recruit other people to sell as your sub-agents and nobody seems particularly interested if any of the innovative revolutionary product or service is ever actually sold.

Be aware that the Internet is changing and will continue to change the way most goods and services are sold. You can open your eyes and harness the Internet's power or blindly pre-tend that it doesn't exist. Many direct sales jobs are being elimi-nated as a consequence of on-line ordering efficiencies. Companies have much to gain from switching from a traditional sales force to an inter-active Internet based sales strategy. Unlike a salesperson, a website doesn't require support, desk space, salaries, commissions or benefits.

OWN YOUR OWN BUSINESS

If you have ever dreamed about owning your own business, then you will want to take the 30-lesson entrepreneurship course called *The Master Small Business Course* on our website at MasterSuccess.com. The course follows three different busi-ness-building scenarios as characters move through the develop-ment stages that begin with having a dream and culminate in opening the doors to success.

To own your own business, you'll want to love something so much that work won't seem like working. The philanthropist John D. Rockefeller said, *"The road to happiness lies in two sim-ple principles; find what it is that interests you and that you can do well, and when you find it put your soul into it – every bit of energy and ambition and natural ability you have."* David

Sarnoff, the founder of RCA, agreed with Rockefeller when he commented, *"Nobody can be successful if he doesn't love his work, love his job."* You won't regret the time that you invest in your business. You won't be afraid to put all the money you've saved to work. You won't mind traveling a hundred miles or a thousand miles to study a business similar to your own where the owner has already achieved the success you desire. You have confidence and aren't easily discouraged. You are good at dealing with people. You like being the boss and assuming the responsibilities of leadership.

David Sarnoff

THE THREE RULES OF BUSINESS

Here are the three steps needed to run a successful small business:

1. Offer a quality product or service that the market demands at a fair price.

2. Appreciate your customer. Always say thank you, ask for feedback and ask for more business.

3. Copy success. Keep improving. Find the people who are doing what you want to do and do what they are doing.

If you do this, the odds for success are with you.

THINK LIKE A REBEL

Should you own your own business? As you first consider your options, beware the naysayers who, in your interest or their own, will immediately throw cold water on your plans.

Some may tell you:

"No, this is the dumbest idea that you've ever come up with. Don't quit your wonderful fry cook job. Doesn't the boss keep telling you that you are one of the best fry cooks that he's ever seen?"

"Don't be foolish. If your idea were any good, someone would have already done it."

"There are enough restaurants."

"No one needs another Internet search engine."

"No one wants home food delivery."

"Your designs aren't that different from everyone else's."

"No one plays the piano anymore."

"You don't have enough education, money, talent or experi-

ence. Stop daydreaming!"

No, start daydreaming!

Those who love you the most will often be the most cautious. They don't want to see you fail and be hurt. They want you to stick with the known, the status quo, and keep frying potatoes

another six weeks, six months, six years. You can't allow yourself to become hypnotized by excuses, either your own or from others. The 18th century English author Dr. Samuel Johnson wrote, *"Nothing will ever be attempted if all possible objections must first be overcome."* You can't allow others to tap into your self-doubt and lull you into complacency. It will always be easy to listen to excuses and quit. Instead, be bold.

Dr. Samuel Johnson

Every successful business started small from some rebel's mind and grew through action. Start your own personal revolution and keep fighting.

IMITATION BEFORE INNOVATION

See what others have done. See what you can do. Copy it. In general, you want to stick closely to the tested and tried and true as possible. After you are established, there will be plenty of time for you to innovate and try new ideas. Remember that you are an entrepreneur and not an inventor. When you invent things, you double your challenges. You first have to convince people that they actually want your new or better something. Then, even if you succeed at the convincing, you have to make them buy from you.

As you think about entrepreneurial opportunities, don't forget any networks or connections that may give you an advantage in starting your own business. Did you acquire skills working as a child in a family business? Can you take over an established family business? Does your uncle or your neighbor or your brother-in-law or a former classmate have connections to assist your business? Somebody you know probably knows somebody who would be willing to give you special assistance because of a personal contact. Build positive business networks. Associate with others committed to self-improvement and helping others. You can go far by yourself and even farther with the help of other people. This is what the Master Success System is all about. Who will help you? Who will take an interest in your career? As you become more and more successful, you will have increasingly greater needs for a good lawyer, banker, investment advisor, real estate agent, accountant, contractor and a host of others. Find them now. Ask people whom you trust for recommendations. Are there Master Success group meetings in your area? Go to MasterSuccess.com and find out.

Most successful small business owners are on a mission. They love their ideas and are full of optimism. Risks really don't seem like risks. Failure isn't on their minds. They have lots of self-confidence. If you're overly concerned about starting your business, you may not be entrepreneurial material.

Many new businesses fail from a lack of planning and from unrealistic expectations. Start small and learn as you grow. The highest probability for success is a business with few employees. If you are a sole proprietor, working alone, you only have to worry about yourself. If you are starting with the obligation to meet a staff payroll, you have to worry about what you have to do and what others have to do. It is easier to be a successful electrician, tailor, graphic designer or landscaper working for yourself than to open a full service restaurant.

THE BOSS'S JOB

If you are an entrepreneur, are you willing to assume your leadership role? The livelihoods of many may rest on your shoulders. You have to understand that your primary role may be as a rainmaker. A rainmaker is the person in the company who brings in new business. In a small business, someone has to bring in the customers. Guess who? The owner of the landscaping company may enjoy mowing lawns but someone has to find the lawns to mow. The lawyer needs clients. The chiropractor needs patients. The caterer needs functions. Your business needs business. If you own a house painting company, you may want to work on the crew with the guys but your real job is knocking on doors and always trying to get the next job. If you own a tool rental business, it may be tough to get on the phone and get the tools back on time. You may have to walk the diplomatic fine line to be able to call people who owe the company money while not alienating someone who may still be a good future customer. If you own a restaurant, you may want to cook, but your real job is to make sure that people come in the front door, love their meals and want to come back for more and bring their friends. As the boss, you must be prepared to assume the responsibility for bringing in the business. This may not be the job that you want to do but until the business is established, marketing may be your primary function.

If you own a business with employees, you need additional social skills. You must be able to plan with a team vision. You must be able to identify individual strengths and get different types of people to work together as a team. You must be able to manage, coordinate, organize and delegate. You must be able to assume responsibility for problems and share the credit for jobs well done. If you are to lead, you must be willing to serve as a role model to employees. You must be the person that you want your employees to be. You must be able to take the extra time to find committed employees who are willing to work to your standards. If you share the Master Success System philosophy, you might want to buy a copy of this book for potential employees. Give them a week to read the book and then have them back for a second interview to discuss the ideas. Only hire people who really want to be hired and show this through their attitude and actions. Are you willing to make this type of investment in your personnel and for your customers? You may find many employees who can lead as well as follow. Consider the advice of Sam Walton, who founded Walmart, *"The key to success is to get out into the store and listen to what the associates have to say. It's terribly important for everyone to get involved. Our best ideas come from clerks and stockboys."*

You can have a website design company. You can have a construction company. You can sell your paintings. You can write books on antiques. You can start a daycare business. You can be a personal trainer. Others have done it. Why not you? Are you working for someone else and feel that you could do just as good or an even better job? Is there a niche in the business you're working in that a new business could fill profitably? What do you think? What are you willing to do about it? Begin your research and never stop.

Look for instances of the 80/20 rule. It pops up a lot. For example, the 80/20 rule says that 80% of your business will come from 20% of your customers. It continues that 80% of your profits will come from 20% of your products.

TESTIMONIALS ARE YOUR BEST ADVERTISEMENTS

Every small business should keep an up to date file of testimonials. Of course, you are going to say that your business is great. What do others say? You want as many customers as possible to become your ambassadors and to spread the good word on your behalf. A testimonial from one regular customer to one prospective customer is worth hundreds of advertising impressions. Your customers, clients, patients and tenants are not statistics. They should be your best salespeople. Since you provide a quality product or service, don't be shy about asking for testimonials.

"Janet Sullivan, the attorney, was so patient and helpful to my mother when she was handling my father's estate."

"I just had my car repainted and the next day I got a big scratch in the door. I brought the car back to All-American Painters and they fixed the scratch for nothing. I can't believe how nice they were."

"My new landscaper, Julio, planted a dozen bulbs in my garden at no charge. When have you ever seen a company do that?"

In these testimonials, you see the basis for successful entrepreneurship. If you can generate this kind of buzz about your business, you will become successful quickly. Be sure to use your testimonials in all your brochures and advertisements. Your potential customers will love to hear others say that you actually do what you say you'll do.

An entrepreneurial spirit is not satisfied with the status quo. If you own a sub shop and are netting a few hundred dollars a week are you content? Or on your free time are you investigating other sub shops even more successful than your own and trying to figure out how you can do what they are doing? What new products or services can you offer? How can you improve? Are you and your staff customer service oriented? How much is your business worth? Would you sell if you got the right offer? Would you open a second location if you saw an opportunity?

Are you aware of trends in your industry? What's selling now and what are the predictions for next year? Do you read industry publications? Surf industry websites? Participate in trade organizations?

If you work for someone else, are you doing so with an

entrepreneurial spirit? Are you working hard for the company, constantly on the lookout for ways to do your job more efficiently, offer new products or services and generally increase productivity and profits?

If you are in business, you must stay current with Internet technology. You must. You can't be left behind. Even if you are a local landscaper, accountant or house cleaner, very soon everyone will turn to your website to learn about your experience, testimonials, services, availability and prices. This is all happening right now. If you can afford to run a successful business, you can afford to build and maintain an on-line presence.

ESTABLISH CLEARLY DEFINED CAREER GOALS

Go right back and review your goals and set your financial course for success. Few successful people are idle or bored. Every day has a specific purpose. Each day brings them one day closer to new heights of achievement. The easiest way to stay focused on your goals is by means of a to-do list. You should think, *"Today is July 31 and this is what I want to accomplish today."* You already know the drill. Commit your goals to writing. Prioritize them. Start with the most important item. Do that. Go to the next item. Working from a to-do list forces you to review and plan. It keeps you on track and helps you to avoid interruptions.

ENJOY YOUR WORK

Being financially successful gives you options. You can do what you want to do. There are 5,000 types of businesses and people have made money at all of them. Ask yourself why this can't be true of you. Successful people generally devote long hours to their work. If you have the choice, choose something that you can enjoy rather than allowing circumstances and luck to rule your life. You can make a million working in any business that you would work in for nothing.

Your career planning must be pro-active and not an afterthought. You don't want to be the person who spends four years in college and tens of thousands of dollars on an education only to end up with all your hopes resting on next Sunday's Help Wanted section of the newspaper. You don't want to be another in the army of college students who major in psychology only to end up in low paying jobs because they didn't take the time to research the likelihood of finding employment as psychology majors.

Enjoying your work gives you a tremendous advantage over your peers. You will want to work at work. Many people don't work very hard at work. Some people are productive only half the time. The rest of the time they are daydreaming, gabbing at the water cooler, taking breaks, going to or from the rest rooms, engaging in personal business or generally doing non-essential activities. Almost all jobs have tedious or arduous aspects to them and it's human nature to avoid these more difficult tasks, even though these are the tasks which may be the most productive for the company. The salesperson doesn't want to have to explain the extended warranty. The auto mechanic doesn't want to make a follow up call to see how the repairs are doing. The real estate agent doesn't want to have to show a house on Sunday night. What others avoid can become your opportunity to profit. This work is your specialty. You know this field much better than most. What can be done faster or better? What gaps need to be filled? Find a niche and fill it.

SURROUND YOURSELF WITH EXCELLENCE

Successful people are goal-oriented. They aren't afraid to work with people who are smarter, harder working or more ambitious than they are. In fact, successful people as managers or entrepreneurs are constantly on the lookout for outstanding performers. If you own a law practice and read a well-researched article by a law student, you may want to invest in a lunch meeting with that student. If you are an entrepreneur, are your competitors good enough to hire, take over or join in a merger? Can you name your most important customers? Are you doing anything special for them? Are you at least in regular communication with them? If not, you are creating an opportunity for your competition.

Encourage dialogue in your organization. If you are hiring workers who subscribe to the Master Success philosophy, you will be working with people who have ideas for improvement. Listen to them even if their ideas may be in conflict with your

own. It is very easy to surround yourself with fawning syco-
phants who take no risks in always agreeing with your *"brilliant
thoughts."* This gets you nowhere. It is much more productive to
engage in honest dialogue and debate with intelligent people
who are not only unafraid but also encouraged to offer their
opinions.

DEVELOP A WINNER'S STYLE AND ATTITUDE

Successful people are doers. Analysis and research are very
important. Listening to others and getting second opinions are

Vincent Van Gogh

very important. Many people get to the point of decision. Then too many people just freeze. They just
keep second-guessing themselves and they allow
their doubts to solidify into inaction. They insist on
guarantees where few exist. Take comfort in the
words of the artist Vincent Van Gogh, *"What would
life be if we had no courage to attempt anything?"*

Even with tons of research, will you always make
the best decisions? If you are on the road to success,
even with the best of intentions, almost certainly not.
Edison failed in 10,000 experiments before inventing the light
bulb. McDonalds is a great franchise, but for over a decade they
introduced one poorly received sandwich after another. Ford
had the Edsel. Bill Gates, the richest man in the world, came to
believe in the Internet very late. Warren Buffett, the second richest man in the world, readily admits that he makes poor stock
picks all the time. Donald Trump is a billionaire but few of his
initial proposals and initial offers go unchallenged. He spends
millions on proposals and projects that amount to nothing. Yet

James Joyce

when he does win, he does so through persistence
and compromise. These companies and businesspeople survive their mistakes. They accept. They learn.
They move on. They are following the words of the
Irish novelist James Joyce, *"Mistakes are the portals of
discovery."* They are following the Action Principles.

Bill Gates invented Windows. Donald Trump built
Trump Tower. Warren Buffett assembled Berkshire
Hathaway. People of action do things. They are persistent and eventually succeed. Right now there are
positive actions that you can take in your life. No one is likely
to run up to you in the street and hand you a big bag of

money. You have to do something. Become self-reliant. Buy a two-family house. Get an MBA. Invest a few thousand and start a small business on the Internet. Study for your real estate license. Even if all you're starting with is a good heart and a burning desire to succeed, you can find many entrepreneurial opportunities. You can incorporate the Action Principles into everything that you do. Starting at this moment, you can become the best you that you can imagine.

BE LIKABLE

Show others that you care. Given a choice, people are going to work harder for and prefer to do business with people they like. If you are an employee, you want tales of your good work habits to reach those in the front offices. If you are an entrepreneur, you want your satisfied customers to become your ambassadors who sing your praises to others. In all areas of business, communication is number one. Keep your clients and customers informed before, during and after the sale. Thank them for their business.

The best reason for a person to do business with you is because you are you. You can earn an MBA but you really only need common sense to know that people like:

Salespeople who follow through.

Clerks who are enthusiastic about their products.

Cashiers who smile and say thank you.

Business owners who give a little more than is expected.

Managers who recognize a job well done.

Contractors who clean up after a job.

Service technicians who listen.

Commit to never-ending improvement. Business knowledge is business power. Keep up with the trade literature in your field. Know and frequent the important websites. Read on-line one of the weekly business magazines or the daily Wall Street Journal. Consider that most of the businesspeople written about are the most successful business people. This is extra work. Do it anyway. Thomas Edison said, *"I never did anything worth doing by accident, nor did any of my inventions come by accident; they came by work."*

Thomas Edison

69

Don't take your employees or customers for granted. The guy who owns the small pizza shop may say that you can't make more than $600 net from a shop like his. Nonsense. He can join both the local Chamber of Commerce and the regional restaurant association and network for new ideas and concepts. He can start visiting other pizza shops doing higher volume to make menu and price comparisons. The woman who works at the library may say that she can't save enough to buy a house and an investment property. She can find a way. She can start reading books on real estate investing and visiting real estate

Tom Brokaw

offices. She can get her real estate license. Other people may not want or be able to do what you can do. Their choice does not have to be your choice. Keep researching your field. Build your self-confidence from a strong knowledge base. Start where you are and start moving. Consider the words of Tom Brokaw, *"It's easy to make a buck. It's a lot tougher to make a difference."* Nelson Mandela was certainly an inspiration when, after thirty years in prison and in his seventies, he didn't choose an easy retirement but rather the presidency of South Africa. He said, *"I can rest but for a moment, for with freedom comes responsibilities, and I dare*

Nelson Mandela

not linger, for my long walk is not ended." How much are you willing to do for yourself and for those you love?

KEY CONCEPTS

To master work you work hard. This doesn't mean burning out working 70 hours a week. Most millionaires only work between 40 to 50 hours a week.

What makes the difference is actually to work while you're working. If there's work that you love doing, do it. Don't do a job you hate. The most successful people are those who love their work.

You must have clearly defined career goals. Choose a career that is exciting to you. Decide whether you want to work for wages or salary, for commission or run your own business. Choose now, before you spend years at college accumulating tons of debt and no marketable skills.

If you work for others, be aware of what opportunities the job offers. If you find yourself in a dead end job you need to change employers. When you find a good employer, as you work always be on the lookout for ways to make yourself more valuable. Those who show persistence and determination and hard work will advance.

If you are working for others, realize that you are not in full control. Pay attention to how the business is doing. If your company is falling behind technologically, losing money, or in a dying industry then you need to look into other options. Conversely, if your company is growing you need to look for ways to ride the wave all the way to the top.

In commissioned sales, if you have the courage to talk convincingly to customers about buying a quality product or service at a fair price, your success is assured. In sales, every person you meet is a potential customer or lead. Learn all you can about your product or service. Learn all you can about your customer's needs. The best salespeople believe in their product or service. Make sure you can really believe in yours.

If you choose to succeed in small business offer a quality product or service that is in demand and charge a fair price. Appreciate your customer. Copy success. Keep improving. Find the people who are doing what you want to do, watch what they do and do it yourself. Ignore the naysayers. If what you want to do has been done, it can be done again – by you! Stick with the tested and tried and true.

Make use of any networks or connections that give you an advantage. Start small and learn by doing. The fewer employees, the lower your overhead and the less can go wrong. If you are a sole proprietor you have a minimum of worries. Be realistic in your expectations.

A great worker studies the great. Find the best, observe them and talk to them. Most will be glad to share what they know. Then, when you know what to do, go out and do it.

Do this and you are sure to master work.

Your Assignment

Your assignment for this chapter is to write a one page Master Work Mission Statement that clearly states the career you have chosen, the level of accomplishment you intend to reach, how much you will earn and the hard work that you are willing to do in exchange. Put your future in writing. This will be a defining moment.

CHAPTER FIVE
MASTER MONEY

The only way to enjoy anything in this life is to earn it first.
Ginger Rogers, American actress & dancer (b. 1911)

Now it's time to take control of your finances. In the previous chapters you have set goals and made plans to achieve those goals. Now, let's take a look at budgeting and investing.

Too many people have too few funds invested for retirement. They spend all of their income, or worse, they find themselves sucked into a downward spiral of debt. Few will be able to enjoy early retirement. In fact, for some, as mentioned, retirement will never come. This spend-it-all-now lifestyle is not just confined to people of modest means. Many people with good incomes who could be wealthy with planning and self-discipline allow themselves to be caught in the same debt trap. They become addicted to immediate gratification and they sentence themselves to a life of toil.

Regardless of your present financial condition, you can master your money. If you faithfully follow The Master Success System, you will be able to maintain a quality lifestyle as you invest for your future. Mastering money requires both persistence and determination.

If you are currently in debt, you need a practical plan to pay down your balances. You must be honest with yourself, acknowledge your problem and show the courage to make changes. As soon as possible, you want to regain control over your financial life. You want to establish and maintain a good credit standing.

The secret to mastering money isn't secret. It is a conscious choice to spend less than you make. It is thinking long term rather than short term. It is realizing that you make money by working hard and investing, and not by applying for new credit cards or other consumer loans. Immediate gratification is alluring. A comfortable early retirement must be even more alluring.

5 SIMPLE STEPS TO MASTERING MONEY

1. Determine how much money you earn now

How much money do you make now? Review your tax return from last year. Subtract the taxes from your total income and you will know your take home pay. If your financial situation has changed substantially since last year, you can calculate your estimated taxes for the current year using the tables available from your local, state and federal government.

2. Calculate how much money you need now

How much money do you need each year? Start by calculating how much you spend each year. To get a clearer picture of your expenses, keep a financial record. Your record can be as simple as a piece of paper or a computerized list of expenses. There are software programs such as Quicken that do an excellent job of cataloging and analyzing personal expenses if you are disciplined about entering the data.

By carefully tracking your expenses for a month you should be able to come up with a good estimate of your annual expenses.

3. Calculate your current net worth

To determine your net worth simply add up your total savings, investments (stocks, bonds, CDs) and assets. At MasterSuccess.com there is a net worth calculator that will take you through this process step by step. Your current net worth provides a starting point for calculating your potential investment returns over time.

4. Estimate the money you'll need to accumulate through savings and investments

How much do you need to make to achieve your goals? Stick to the big ticket items: primary residence, vacation home, investment property, tuition, cars, boats, retirement, etc. What is the approximate amount of money you would need to have in investments? For example, if you had $600,000 invested with an 8% return, you would generate $48,000 in income before taxes or $38,000 after taxes. These are big numbers. However, if you start saving early, through the wonder of compound interest, your assets will appreciate substantially. Start somewhere. Save something. Be disciplined and persistent. Go to MasterSuccess.com and try different savings and investment scenarios using the compound interest calculator. By entering your current net worth, your financial goal and estimated rates of return, you will be able to determine realistic financial goals. By varying the amount you save each year you'll see that small changes can, over time, translate into large differences in future outcomes.

5. Devise a specific plan to earn and save enough money to reach your goal

As you create your budget you should keep in mind the following. You must save enough to:

1. Get out of consumer debt, if any.
2. Establish a cash reserve.
3. Invest for retirement.

Because consumer debt is a continuous drain on your income you should make paying down high interest balances your first priority. There's no point in investing money for a return of 12% if you're still paying 19% interest for that flat screen television you bought last year.

The second step is to put aside enough cash to provide a safety net. One good rule to follow is to keep enough money on hand to live for six months. This can also be in the form of cash equivalents rather than a normal savings account in order to benefit from the higher interest rates.

For retirement, your target should be to accumulate a nest egg large enough to provide sufficient annual income to live in the lifestyle to which you have become accustomed. To maintain your current lifestyle in retirement, you will need about 75% - 80% of your working annual income. Don't wait. Start now to estimate your Social Security, annuity and pension plan benefits. Then, you will have a general goal marker to formulate your personal investment program. How much supplementary investment income will you need?

Once or twice a year, you should review your retirement standing and options. Are you forty years from retirement or four years? Will any of your pensions allow for early retirement? Will your personal investment program ever be large enough to allow you to retire at 60, 55 or even younger? How can you modify your lifestyle to make early retirement a more viable option?

Observe and consider that many people who have sufficient resources to retire early don't because they have never taken the time to explore options outside of work. They have allowed their entire identity to be defined by work. They have not given themselves permission to follow the Action Principle, *"Love Many Things."* If you have a lot of money, sit back and enjoy giving it away to those in need. Then, go fishing, paint, read, write, travel or take your grandchildren to the park. And, of course, continue your masterful obligation to teach others so that they may follow in your footsteps. To be a master, you must teach.

SAVING MONEY

Every time you buy something that you don't need you are stealing from yourself. The earlier in life you begin a savings program, the more interest compounding will work to your benefit. Immediately, set a savings goal equal to 10% of your income. Many wealthy people save 20% to 50% of their incomes. As you get older, you will have bought and furnished your house. You will have paid for your children's braces and schooling. You've done these things. You don't have to do them again. You will be able to save increasingly larger percentages of your earnings. This is the mindset of the wealthy. For reference, average Americans currently save about 2% of their incomes.

The best way to start saving is by reducing your spending.

As you keep your financial record, you are becoming a conscious consumer aware of what and why you are buying. Just being aware will often reduce your spending.

One of the largest purchases made by the average American is his car. Many people associate having a nice new car with wealth. Yet studies of self-made millionaires show that most choose to buy moderately priced cars and not luxury models. You can conclude that the habits that lead them to buy practical, reasonably priced cars are a major part of what made them millionaires. The legend of the penny-pinching millionaire is worth considering.

Once you own an expensive object, whether it is a video camera, a home or a car, take care of it. Get that oil changed. Follow the manufacturer's periodic maintenance recommendations. Put the lens cap on when you're done using it. If the roof springs a leak get it fixed ASAP.

Prepay regular expenses whenever you are offered a substantial discount. Paying your car insurance yearly may save you a significant amount of money. Have you been paying for cable

TV for years? Some cable companies will give you a discount if you prepay your bill.

Do you really need the things you think you need? Is your car a reliable means of transportation or a status symbol? Are you buying for yourself or to impress others? Are you self-confident enough to delay the purchase of the new suit or the new car because you know that your self worth does not come from the approval of others? When you are young is the hardest time to fight the pull of peer approval. Yet, every dollar that you can save when you are young will be compounded again and again on your journey to prosperity. Every dollar that you save and invest at 6% interest will double in twelve years. The formula to determine when your money doubles is to divide the interest rate into 72.

Save every month – pay yourself first. Delay the temptation of immediate gratification and status when you are young and live long and prosper.

If you are an employee and your company offers you a retirement fund with matching contributions take advantage of it. It offers tax savings, tax deferral of investment earnings and, best of all, more money. Many companies will give you thousands of dollars for free if you have a retirement plan. If they have matching contributions, you should take advantage to the maximum allowed.

If you are self employed you should start a SEP-IRA. This individual retirement account for the self employed will allow you to shelter as much as 15% of your income until you retire. Again, your goal is to save and invest at least 10% of your income.

The rules governing IRAs are very complex. You will have to research them carefully in order to come up with a plan that is best for you. Be sure to check MasterSuccess.com for links to detailed information on this and many other financial subjects.

There will be some people who, even after they have gone through the exercises in this chapter, carefully analyzed their budget and cut expenses down to the bone, still find that they don't earn enough money to reach their financial goals. If that describes you, now is the time to consider switching to a higher paying career or getting a second job or working overtime. Find a way. Do what you have to do. For too many, Social Security is their retirement cake. For you, make sure that Social Security is only the icing.

Avoid consumer debt

Consumer debt is the opposite of investment. Investment compounds gain while debt compounds loss. Consumer debt means you are falling behind in the wealth accumulation game. Consumer debt should not be confused with borrowing to invest in a business or financing the purchase of assets that appreciate such as real estate. The last thing you want is to pay 19% interest on a credit card purchase of an *'asset'* that is depreciating by 25% every year! If you currently have a lot of consumer debt and you own a home, you should think about using a home equity loan to pay off your credit card debt. This will generally lower your interest rate. This strategy will only work if you are prepared to change your financial lifestyle. As you wipe the slate clean and get some debt relief, you can't continue with the same spending patterns that got you into trouble in the first place. Learn from your mistakes. Be wiser the next time around.

Credit Cards

Every adult needs a credit card. Preferably, you will search for a good deal, which usually means a card with a low fixed interest rate. You want a low annual interest rate and not a free toaster or tote bag. Beware of low introductory rates. They will lure you in and then hope that you won't notice or be too lazy to switch when the rate skyrockets in six months. For more consumer tips, make frequent visits to MasterSuccesss.com.

Investments Explained

There are four basic areas where you should consider investing your money. They are cash equivalents, stocks, bonds and real estate. Mutual funds are a diversified method for investing in stocks and bonds. Real estate is an excellent investment and will be covered in detail in the next chapter.

Investing in gold, collectibles or commodities futures takes specialized knowledge and is not a wise choice unless you have or are willing to acquire the necessary expertise. Gold is an inflation hedge – that is, when inflation is high the real price of gold tends to go up relative to other goods and services. The trouble with gold is that inflation has been low for over a decade and shows no sign of making a comeback. So barring the return of inflation, it would be best to avoid gold unless you are an economist or gold specialist.

Collectibles are often perishable and you have to have years of specialized knowledge in the field to properly evaluate each individual type. Different types of collectibles can also quickly be in and out of favor. From modern art to baseball cards, you have to be very careful if you are buying as an investor rather than a hobbyist.

Speculating in the commodities futures market will always be a high-risk venture for the average investor. Commodities are often a gamble for the pros and high rollers who have enough of a stake to diversify and offset losses.

Money Market Funds

These funds are a special category of mutual fund. They invest only in cash equivalents. Cash equivalents are debt instruments that mature in a year or less. These include T-Bills, CDs and commercial paper. The fund earns interest on these investments and distributes the interest to investors daily. These funds are extremely liquid. You can write checks on them just as you would on a normal checking account.

CDs (Certificates of Deposit)

CDs are certificates from a bank or savings and loan showing that they have received from the person named a sum of money as a deposit. CDs pay interest for a specific time period. As the owner of a CD you get regular interest payments, and when the CD matures you get back the amount you invested. The upside is they allow you to lock in interest rates for the term of the CD and because they are covered by federal deposit insurance, they are very safe.

Treasury Bills (T-Bills)

T-Bills are short-term government issued debts. They mature within 13, 26 or 52 weeks – that is they are repaid in full within that timeframe. The minimum face value available is $10,000. They are also available at larger face values in $5,000 increments. T-Bills are sold at a discount of the face value. The interest is the difference between the price paid and the face value. T-Bills usually pay about 1% less than large bank CDs. While they are one of the least risky places to keep your money, they offer mediocre returns. Since 1926 they have appreciated an average of 3.8% annually.

Bonds

Bonds are IOUs issued by governments and companies. When you buy a bond you are lending money to the issuer. You collect regular interest payments until the money is returned. In most cases this is a fixed percentage of the bond's face value. A bond's 'maturity' is the date that the bondholder will get back the original investment.

A bond's 'coupon' is its annual interest rate. So a bond with a 6.50% coupon has an annual interest rate of 6.50%. Bonds are not as profitable as stocks during good times but they are much safer during bad times. The tradeoff is security. If you buy government bonds you are never – barring some complete disaster – going to lose all your money. In part the decision comes down to your temperament. How much risk are you comfortable with? It makes no sense to invest in something that is going to keep you up nights worrying.

Treasury Bonds

US government bond maturities range between 11 and 30 years. They are backed by the full faith and credit of the US government so they are one of the safest investments. The prices of existing bonds relate directly to current interest rates. If the interest rate goes up the prices of bonds fall to remain competitive with new issues offering a better return. If interest rates decline the market price of existing bonds paying higher rates will rise.

Municipal Bonds

Tax free municipal bonds (also known as 'munis') are issued by cities in the United States. They have special legal status which means you pay no federal or state taxes on the interest they pay. That's the plus side. The downside is they generally pay a lower interest rate. If you are in a low tax bracket they usually aren't a very attractive investment. Of course, given the prosperity that you will soon enjoy from following the Master Success System, municipal bonds may be in your future.

Mutual Funds

A mutual fund is a company that invests on your behalf. Mutual funds sell shares, which give you a share of the fund and voting rights proportionate to your share. Each mutual fund publishes a prospectus which explains the fund's investment policies, risks, costs, turnover rate (to what extent they buy and sell assets each year) and past performance. Nearly 40% of

Americans have some money invested in mutual funds.

The primary advantage of a mutual fund is diversification. When you buy into a fund, with one purchase you are investing in a variety of companies. As with stocks, you can sell your shares of the fund at any time. There are over 10,000 different funds.

There are over 10,000 different mutual funds. Here are broad categories:

General Equity Funds

These are funds that invest in stocks. These funds are often classified by the sort of stocks they buy. The three primary types are Value, Growth or the combination of those two known as Blend.

Funds also categorize stocks by their market capitalization, also known as market cap. There are three types: small cap, medium cap and large cap. Market capitalization is the current value of a company's stock shares. To calculate this you just multiply the current price by the number of shares. Small caps are worth between $100 and $500 million, mid caps are worth between $500 million and $5 billion and large caps are worth $5 billion or more.

There are funds which invest chiefly in one of these types and are thus known as small, medium or large cap funds. Over time smaller companies have shown higher returns so the theory is that small cap funds have a higher upside potential.

Bond Funds

These funds invest their money in bonds. The advantages and disadvantages of such funds are pretty much the same as when you buy bonds yourself. There's not a lot of risk but not the best return either.

Balanced Funds

These funds invest in a mix of stocks and bonds. Most have between 50-65% stocks with the rest in bonds. When selecting a balanced fund make sure you know the specific proportion so you can properly evaluate the relative risk.

Sector Funds

These are funds that invest in specific types of stocks – high tech, finance, manufacturing, consumer electronics, etc. Sector funds can fluctuate in value considerably as the fortunes of its favored sector rise and fall. Most experts do not recommend sector funds for beginning investors.

International Funds

International funds invest only in countries outside of the United States. They tend to be a lot more volatile than other types of funds. There are also 'Global Funds' which can invest some of their money in the United States.

Index Funds

An index fund purchases shares of stock based on a particular index such as the S&P 500. These funds reproduce the performance of the index exactly. The upside of these funds is that they tend to have low overhead since all they do is buy and hold the indexed stocks. The downside is they will not have the high performance of riskier funds.

WHEN CHOOSING A FUND YOU SHOULD FOLLOW THESE RULES:

Read the prospectus

The prospectus gives you the information you need to determine whether the fund is even worth taking a chance on. By reading it you will be able to see how much it has made in the past and estimate how much the fund is likely to make in the future. You will also find a discussion of the fund's investment strategy.

Choose only no load funds

The fund's *loads* are basically commissions or sales charges. Front end loads are charges you must pay when buying into a fund. Back end loads are charges you must pay when selling the fund. Since there is no evidence showing that funds that charge these fees are any more profitable than those that do not they are bad news and should be avoided.

The fund's expense ratio should be below 1%

This is the ratio of assets to annual fees. These include management fees, administrative costs and other operating expenses. You want a fund that is as efficiently managed as possible since this comes out of your profit.

Choose a fund with an investment strategy you are comfortable with

The prospectus will explain the fund's objectives and how they intend to reach them. If you wouldn't feel comfortable investing in futures yourself it's a good idea to avoid investing in a fund that will do it on your behalf.

Choose a fund that is likely to outperform the stock market

If your fund does not outperform the market you'd be better off with a simple index fund. www.morningstar.net has charts that show how well a fund has done relative to the market over time.

STOCKS

You may be surprised to learn that stocks not only provide the highest potential returns over the long haul but that they are also relatively safe. The key phrase is *'the long haul.'* If you buy an assortment of stocks and hold them for 20 years you are almost certain to make money. If you have the discipline to stick to your plan you will beat the majority of day traders who jump from one investment to another in hopes of hitting the jackpot.

BUY WHAT YOU KNOW

Warren Buffett and Peter Lynch, two of the world's most successful stock pickers, recommend that investors buy what they know. If your work gives you expertise in a particular area, make use of that specialized knowledge and you can often outperform the market. If you're an auto dealer, invest in auto companies and their parts suppliers. If you're a computer programmer, invest in promising computer companies. If you have a hobby, consider investing in companies involved in your avocation. If you love movies and you think one movie studio is going to do particularly well, buy stock in the company. If you are into running and have a chance to talk to other runners and evaluate products, you may want to buy stock in sporting goods manufacturers or retailers.

But what if you don't believe you have special knowledge that lends itself to investing? Chances are you really do! Even without in depth knowledge from your career or hobbies you can still make use of knowledge from your experience as a consumer. If a particular chain store where you shop has great service and is publicly traded then you could do worse than to buy some stock in it. If your kids are obsessed with video games, you might want to consider buying some video game company stock.

Before purchasing any stock be sure to get some perspective

on how it has performed recently. The Internet makes this very easy. If you want to invest in stocks, it is essential to have a computer and Internet access. The discounted savings you make in broker fees by trading electronically may be enough to pay for the computer. The principal reason to use a full service broker is for information and advice. However, if you go the discount route, you are strictly on your own.

Stocks offer the potential for sizeable long-term gains but unlike government bonds there are no guarantees. If a company you own stock in goes bankrupt your shares will become virtually worthless. That's why research is so important before you invest.

Many new investors prefer buying blue chip stocks. Blue chip stocks are shares of large established companies. Blue chip stocks have earned an average of 11% annually for the past 72 years presuming you reinvested the dividends. If you wish to buy shares yourself – as opposed to selecting a mutual fund primarily invested in stocks - the simplest way is to buy an assortment of blue chip stocks. For most people, investing in stocks with a long-term slow and steady strategy is best. Buy stocks you believe in and hold on to them. Be patient. Don't rush to sell every time there is a market correction. This not only avoids the anxiety of trading but also saves on commissions.

CHOOSING YOUR STRATEGY

As an investor you are often balancing risk versus reward. For example, cash equivalents have yielded about 4.2% annually since 1900. Long term government bonds have yielded about 4.0% annually during the same period. Stocks have yielded an average of 9.8% annually since 1900.

Remember that these averages are just that – they don't show the extreme fluctuations underlying these numbers. In the 1950s bonds performed miserably while in the 1980s they were outstanding. And while stocks are doing splendidly now, investors in 1929 could take small comfort in the fact that the coming depression was an exception to the bullish 20th century trend. More recently, in 1987 the market lost 1/4th of its value in a single day! There are investors who lose money every day no matter how well the overall market is performing. All it takes is choosing the wrong stocks. Many investors minimize risk by purchasing shares of an index fund rather than betting everything on a few companies. Be conservative in your planning and count on no more than the 10% average return.

How do you invest?

Here are some basic principles to guide your investing.

Knowledge is power. Learn all you can. Thanks to the Internet there is now a wealth of information that is free or nearly free and is available to everyone. You need to be aware of what is happening today. There are resources to help you keep up to date about this on our web site, MasterSuccess.com.

Stick to your plan. If your goal requires that you save $50 a week, save $50 a week. Don't change your strategy every time you read an article or hear a gloomy forecast on the evening news. If the market has a bad week just keep cool. Take comfort in the fact that you are in for the long term. Time is your ally.

Remember that your return on the investment is how much you make after you take all taxes and fees into account as well as adjusting for inflation. High fees at any stage can turn apparent profit into actual loss. Always consider the transaction costs when comparing investment alternatives.

One of the most important rules to follow as you are building wealth is to reinvest your returns. When stocks pay dividends, use these profits to buy more stocks. When you collect interest roll it right back into your portfolio.

Hold on to what you've got. The most successful investors are those who choose their investments carefully and then stick with them. Market timing – trying to buy when the market hits bottom and sell when it peaks – is very difficult. There are links to electronic brokers on MasterSuccess.com.

There is no substitute for your own judgement based upon your own research. Before you give anyone any money, know precisely which commissions and fees are your responsibility. Patience pays. Compound interest favors those who show persistence and the more persistence they show the greater the rewards. Get rich quick plans almost always fail. Get rich slow almost always works.

Retirement Plans

In addition to building up your nest egg there are several

ways to save for your retirement and avoid taxes. You don't have to be a millionaire to take advantage of tax shelters. At this writing the following methods allow you to save and invest money tax deferred:

Individual Retirement Accounts (IRAs)

An IRA allows you to invest up to $2000 annually tax deferred. While that may not seem like much to some, the wonders of compound interest can make it quite substantial over time. An IRA may be invested in several ways including stocks, bonds and money market accounts.

Simplified Employee Pension (SEP-IRA)

An IRA set up by an employer. An employer may contribute up to $30,000 or 15% of an employee's compensation annually to the employee's IRA.

Keogh Plans

If you have a business these plans permit you to defer paying taxes on up to 25% of your salary which can then be placed in this fund and invested. The upside of this is that you can contribute a great deal more than with any other plan. The downside is that it involves a lot of complicated paperwork to file.

Deferred Annuities

Deferred annuities are contracts issued to an investor by an insurance company, generally in exchange for a single payment. The annuity provides lifetime payments to the investor starting at some point in the future. Until that time the annuity earns and accumulates investment income without being taxed. Deferred annuities generally earn interest at a rate that fluctuates with market interest rates. The rates are not locked in – the insurance company can pay what it likes – but they must pay a competitive rate to prevent investors from closing out their annuities. You can decide to close out the annuity at any time, taking all your money in a lump sum. When you do

"Winning is crucial to my retirement plans."

so, you must pay a tax on the accumulated income.

Variable Annuities

A variable annuity is a specific type of deferred annuity. Earnings on variable annuities also accumulate tax-free. But a variable annuity's value varies based upon the rise or fall of the stocks or bonds in which the annuity is invested. When choosing a variable annuity be aware that the fees charged often offset the tax benefits.

When planning for retirement keep in mind that the closer you are to retiring the less risk you can afford. It is one thing to invest heavily in stocks in your thirties and be hit by a market crash. After all, the overall long-term historical trend is that the market is headed up. However if you're just five years from retirement, it may not trend upward soon enough for you to recover from your losses! So a good rule is to reduce the proportion of your portfolio allocated to volatile investments as you get older.

LIFE INSURANCE

You should purchase life insurance if any of your loved ones would suffer a financial loss as a result of your death. The amount of insurance you should buy is entirely based on how many people depend on you. You will need more insurance if you are married with children and one parent works at home. Most people are insured for three times their annual income. You should base how much insurance you buy on your family's specific financial needs.

There are several types of life insurance. Ordinary life insurance is usually sold in units of $1,000. It may provide a single lump sum payment or continuing income to the beneficiaries. Companies may also elect to insure the life of a valuable employee. In most cases (other than term life insurance) ordinary life insurance builds value that can be borrowed against in emergencies.

Whole-life insurance pays the face amount of the policy upon the death of the insured. Premiums are paid throughout the life of the insured person.

Limited-payment life insurance, as the name implies, charges premiums for a limited number of years unless the insured dies prior to the specified limit. A single payment policy is a specific case of a limited-payment policy. Premiums for limited-payment policies are higher than for ordinary life insurance since the payments are made over a shorter time period.

Endowment insurance is payable upon the death of the insured or at a specified date (the date of maturity) provided the insured remains alive. Premiums are, in most cases, paid from the date of issue until the date of maturity. However they can be limited to a shorter time or even made in a single lump sum payment. Premiums are high because of the short time frame. These policies combine elements of savings and insurance. They can be used for education, retirement or to make mortgage payments. However, higher yields available from other investments make this option uncompetitive.

Cash value policies such as whole life, endowment and limited payment life must provide the cash surrender value of the policy if the insured terminates it.

Term life insurance only pays benefits if the insured dies within a specific timeframe. If the insured lives to the end of the specified time, the policy is terminated unless it is renewed. Premiums are lower for term policies because it only has to pay benefits if the insured dies within the allotted time. It usually has no cash surrender value. With each renewal, premiums increase because they are based on the age of the insured when the policy is renewed. You also may have to take another medical exam and this may cause premiums to increase even further. Many term insurance policies allow the insured to convert to whole-life policies. You should choose term insurance if you are young and you don't have a lot of money to pay the higher premiums required for other plans.

A specialized form of life insurance is credit life insurance. If the insured takes out a large loan, this insurance protects his or her family from any debt that remains if the insured dies before the loan is repaid.

Group life insurance applies to a number of people in a business or other organization. A contract is issued and each member is given a certificate showing the amount of insurance and the beneficiary. Group life insurance provides economies of scale and the savings are passed on to the insured through lower premiums. These policies include a conversion clause allowing the insured to convert to a nonterm policy upon leaving the organization without requiring a medical examination. It is generally issued on a one year renewable term basis. Because of the potential cost savings you should check to see if you are eligible for group life insurance through your employer or any professional associations you belong to.

PERSISTENCE PAYS

Each year you should redo the financial calculations discussed in this chapter and on the MasterSuccess.com website. You should adjust your plan as you progress towards your goals. If you have a few good years you may be able to move your timetable to retirement forward. A few bad years and you might need to increase the amount you save each month to make up for lost time. You should be flexible while keeping your eyes on the prize.

KEY CONCEPTS

To master money, you must control spending, saving and investing. Devise a realistic budgeting plan that you will follow. You need to determine your income and expenses. You need to save money to reduce debt, establish an emergency cash reserve and invest for retirement. Share this plan with all family members and give everyone an opportunity to do his or her part and understand the future benefits.

Spend less than you make. Frugality should be encouraged and taught to loved ones and employees. Save 10% of your income.

To maintain or exceed your current quality of life into your retirement years, you need a long-term investment plan. You must determine and account for your insurance needs including medical and long term care, housing needs, ordinary expenses and leisure costs. Look to your pensions, inheritances, savings, retirement plans and real estate investments for solutions. The best time to draft and begin implementing this plan is immediately. You want to begin investing as early as possible to take maximum benefit of compound interest.

Most people don't have a plan and too many not a clue. As a member of the Master Success System, you are different. Study, plan and act. Financial planning should be a priority to ensure a smooth, pleasant life journey.

YOUR ASSIGNMENT

Your assignment for this chapter is to start saving. Even if you can only put aside a small amount, begin today. You will be establishing a good habit that will last a lifetime. You will know that you're moving in the right direction. You should commit to saving at least 10% of your income. As soon as you get paid, set aside this money. Start a savings account until you have saved enough to begin a serious investment program. Keep saving.

Chapter Six
Master Real Estate

*I know the price of success: dedication, hard work, and
an unremitting devotion to the things you want to see happen.*
Frank Lloyd Wright, American Architect (b. 1867)

In the last two chapters, you learned the style and attitudes
best suited to making a living. Now, let's go to a whole different
level. In the next few pages, you are going to learn how to
make money in real estate. For most people, this means buying
a home and waiting for it to appreciate. That's OK. However,
the information in this chapter can be much more useful. This
information can be your bridge to early retirement or to realize
many personal dreams.

Here are a few reasons you should be interested in real estate
investing:

• More money has been made in real estate than in all other
investments combined.

• Real estate deals involve tens and hundreds of thousands of
dollars, which means that even small percentage gains when
buying or selling can yield substantial profits.

• You don't have to own a lot of real estate to become financially secure.

• There is a lot of real estate and that means a lot of opportunities.

• Prices are very subjective.

• You can control large investments with small percentage
downpayments.

• Simple research can make you a pricing expert in a short
period of time.

The real estate investment system described in this chapter
and further in the *Master Real Estate Course* offered at
MasterSuccess.com will work anywhere. It works in Boston,
Houston, Santiago, Chile or a small village in France. With

patience, it works all the time. You can start the system with a few thousand dollars or a million. Your research will limit your risk. Your profits will continue to grow as you continue to use the system and inflation raises values. The system works if you buy one house in your life or six houses every year. Some people may even choose to make real estate investing their careers.

Understanding the real estate market is a must for anyone seeking financial independence. Residential real estate transactions in the United States represent a $1 trillion business or 15% of the country's total gross national product. The Internet as a real estate investing tool is becoming increasingly useful. Presently, there are over a quarter of a million real estate websites. For the latest real estate investment information, education and links, make frequent visits to MasterSuccess.com.

PRICE, PRICE, PRICE

What's the most important rule to follow when making money in real estate? The standard answer is location, location, location.

This is the wrong answer.

The correct answer is price, price, price.

If you are willing to think unconventionally for the next hour as you read and digest the information in this chapter, you will begin to see how the world of real estate actually works. You will see that the real estate business works just like any other business. To make a profit, you must buy low and sell high.

The conventional wisdom espoused by many in the real estate profession is that you can't do this. Because they haven't done it, they want you to believe that making money in real estate is somehow different from making money in other kinds of businesses.

This is wrong.

You can buy and sell and buy and sell over and over again. You can make a profit on each transaction. The system couldn't be more logical or uncomplicated. The ease of the system makes you wonder why more people aren't real estate investors.

Let's begin.

You buy a mansion in a fantastic location for a million dollars. If the mansion is worth a million dollars, you make no money. It's worth a million and you pay a million. So, instead of buying the mansion you buy a rundown two-family house in a bad location. This property is actually worth $60,000 but you buy it for $40,000. How do you know that the property is worth $60,000? Because you have made the effort to research prices. Why did you get such a deal? There could be many many possible reasons. One of these reasons will simply be that you made an offer and that offer was accepted. You made an offer to an owner who wanted to sell and no one else made an acceptable offer before you did.

This is very straightforward.

If you told your friends about buying the mansion, they would ooh and ah in admiration and offer their congratulations. If you told them about buying the dilapidated two-family – well, they might be very happy to recite every horror story and bad problem that they ever had with real estate. If they haven't had any, they will repeat every bad experience that they've ever heard of – the pipes leaking, the tenants from hell, the junk cars, the vacancies, etc., etc. Of course, all of these bad things could be among the good reasons why you were able to buy the property for $40,000. For the $20,000 profit, you'd have to be willing to correct the problem and call a plumber, a lawyer, a tow truck or a rental agent. In the final analysis, you may never find out the seller's exact motivation in accepting your offer. The reasons could be business or personal. You offered $35,000 and then $38,000 and then your $40,000 offer was accepted. Does the reason the seller decided to accept your offer really matter?

BUY. SELL. PROFIT.

What if you don't want to own the two-family? You sell it. You take your profit and you buy something that you do want to own. Don't allow the details to obscure the larger picture. Is there a guarantee that you can sell the house for $60,000 that

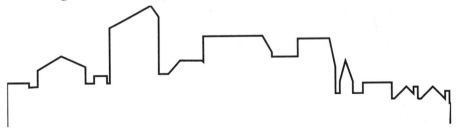

you buy for $40,000? Of course not. The $60,000 price is your best estimate after you buy it, maybe clean it up and resell. There are no guarantees and that is the main reason that most people don't have the courage to take a risk. They would prefer a guarantee. You can find investments that are guaranteed but the investment returns are minimal. The Master Success System is giving you the courage to do more, to build confidence. You research. You make offers. You buy. You sell. You profit.

What happens if after you buy the property that you decide to rent it rather than sell it? Sure, why not?

Is the point to buy junk property? No, the point to is buy real estate for less than what it is worth. You buy real estate for less than what it's worth by researching and becoming an expert at value and by making offers. The examples of the run down property and the mansion are illustrative of the concept. The location doesn't matter. The type of property doesn't matter. The price matters. The price allows you the leeway to buy, hold and resell at a net profit after expenses including capital gains taxes.

Beware of fixer-uppers. Fixer-uppers are houses in need of repair. Fixer-uppers are not automatically good deals. In fact, if you aren't a professional contractor, they can be money pits and very bad deals. Stick to making a reasonable profit based on your research, your negotiating skills and your willingness to make offers.

REAL ESTATE AND PENCILS

Let's compare real estate to the pencil business. You are in the pencil business and your standard pencil sells for an average price of $0.10. Some fancy stores sell the pencil for $0.12 and some discounters sell it for $0.08. You are the pencil manufacturer. To make a profit of $0.02 per pencil, you must get a wholesale price of $0.06 per pencil.

Who cares if one guy makes one cent on a pencil and another guy makes three cents on a pencil and someone makes two cents on a pencil? Who cares about pencils? The point of the pencil analogy is to help you to gain insight into the real estate investment business. You can do the same thing with real estate that the pencil guy does with his pencils. The difference is that his pencil may cost $0.10 and your real estate may cost $100,000. He makes a couple of pennies and you make thou-

sands. If someone can make 10%- 20% margins buying and selling pencils, you can make 10% -20% margins buying and selling
real estate. The business principles of buying at wholesale
prices and selling at retail prices are the same.

Actually this isn't totally correct because investing and making
money in residential real estate can be a lot easier than being in
the pencil business. In the pencil business, all of the parties
involved: the manufacturer, the wholesaler and the retailer are
certainly very knowledgeable about pencil values. In contrast, in
residential real estate, you may be dealing with a seller who has
little personal knowledge of value who is being advised by an
agent who may not know much more. In many residential transactions, your specialized knowledge of value will give you a
clear advantage when you negotiate.

If you were buying stocks, would you ever invest through a
stockbroker who never bought stocks for himself? Of course
not. Then, why would you choose to work with a real estate
agent who never bought investment real estate? In fact, very few
real estate agents own investment real estate. It may be difficult
for you to find a residential investment agent in your community. The obvious reason is that the agents who buy investment
real estate make enough money that they don't have to be real
estate agents any more. Being a real estate broker can be a
tough job.

THE RESIDENTIAL REAL ESTATE MARKETING PROCESS

The average piece of residential real estate is sold every seven
years. This means that in their lifetimes, most sellers will be
involved in fewer than ten transactions. This is a minimal
amount of real estate activity with most transactions spaced
years apart.

The purchase and sale of a home are usually the largest financial transactions in which anyone is ever involved. You would
think that any rational person would seek expert assistance to
protect their most valuable asset. The person called is a real
estate agent.

The next step in our system is to understand the role of real
estate agents: what they do and how they do it.

Where do homeowners select a real estate agent? Did they see a yard sign? Is it the agent that they used seven years ago? Is it their niece? Did they see a warm and fuzzy TV commercial? Did they simply walk into an office nearest their home?

After twenty years or more of study, all brain surgeons are probably pretty good brain surgeons. If you meet someone who is a board certified brain surgeon, she is probably a pretty good brain surgeon.

If you meet someone and they tell you that they are a board-certified real estate agent, there is less certainty that they are good real estate agents. In many places, becoming a real estate agent is not exactly the result of rigorous study. If you are a high school graduate, haven't been convicted of a felony, take a few classes and pass a simple test, you are in the business.

Again, there are smart agents. The smartest real estate agents are those who quickly figure out that the best reason to be in the real estate business is to scoop up the best bargains for themselves before the general public can get to them. The smart real estate agent quickly becomes the smart real estate investor.

There are also superstar real estate agents who make six figure incomes. With a little research, you can find and cultivate these agents. They will understand your system. They will not be offended by your fondness for making offers because they will be smart enough to see beyond a single transaction to you as a client who will generate multiple commissions.

Average real estate agents, many of whom are part-timers, are the guiding forces behind most residential real estate transactions in America.

THE HIGH COST OF FREE

In a typical transaction, the residential sales process begins with a homeowner requesting a *"Free Market Analysis."* It is hard to imagine that a homeowner who is about to enter into a financial transaction involving hundreds of thousands of dollars would opt to let the appraisal rest on a *"Free Market Analysis."* Incomprehensibly, it seems that most homeowners rationalize that it would be foolish to spend a few hundred dollars on an independent professional appraisal when the local real estate agent is willing to do the job for nothing.

This is a big mistake. However, it is a mistake that only creates more opportunities for you.

The real estate agent answering the phone is always highly motivated. She is motivated to get the listing. The homeowner who calls a real estate agent is not speaking to an independent consultant who will objectively offer advice. Instead, the homeowner is speaking with a commissioned salesperson who needs listings to survive.

Here is a typical house listing scenario.

The agent tours the house while complimenting the homeowners on their decorating expertise. The agent wants to befriend the homeowners and gain their confidence. At this time, the agent will also help the homeowners alleviate any fears they may have about the pending sale. If the homeowners are concerned about the leaking cesspool or the cracked foundation or lead paint, the agent offers comfort. Don't worry. Don't worry. The agent thinks to herself that she will deal with any house problems after she has gotten the listing. Her job is focused on getting the listing. Without the listing, there is nothing.

After the house tour, the agent and homeowners sit down to begin a cat and mouse quiz. The aim of the agent is to try and figure out if the homeowner has a value figure in mind or what number is going to make the homeowner pleasantly surprised. The agent doesn't dare risk insulting the homeowner with a low number. *"Free Market Analysis"* evaluations always start high. If the house doesn't sell, there will be plenty of time to knock the price down at a later date. The agent tells the owner what the owner wants to hear in order to get the listing. The agent needs to get the listing before leaving the house. The agent doesn't want the homeowner to seek a second opinion and run the risk that the second opinion comes in even higher than her inflated figure.

The agent gives the homeowner a value for the house, which ensures that the homeowner gives the agent the listing.

You can hire trained professional independent appraisers who will research sales and give you a detailed analysis of value. This takes some time and costs hundreds of dollars.

Realistically, how much work can a real estate agent offering a *"Free Market Analysis"* afford to do? Maybe she spends a few minutes looking for other similar houses on the market or comparable recent sales. Maybe. The object of the real estate agent is to get the listing and get the house on the market and allow the market, through the eventual buyer, to set the true value.

The incentive of the agent is not to establish value. It is to get the listing.

This is the way most residential real estate transactions work. Are there fantastic real estate agents, knowledgeable sellers and savvy buyers who are exceptions to the above? Of course, there will always be exceptions. Is the point to ridicule real estate agents? Of course not. This system is not about real estate agents. It is about making money in real estate. To make money in real estate, you often have to work with, around, over or under one or two real estate agents.

Every offer you make on a property will not be accepted. In fact, most offers that you make on property will not be accepted. It is only necessary to know that some offers will be accepted and from those accepted offers you will profit handsomely.

You are going to make money in the real estate business because you will be more knowledgeable than the other parties to the transaction. You are going to make money because your expectations are reasonable which may be 10% -20% margins when you are buying or selling.

Let's say that you buy a very ordinary condo that your research tells you is worth $100,000. Every time one of these units comes on the market, you offer $80,000. Sometimes these offers will be rejected outright. Sometimes there will be counter offers. Perhaps, after one of your offers, the real estate agent tells you that the seller has been transferred out of state and is interested in a speedy transaction. This presents a win-win situation for both you and the seller. Since you have your financing pre-arranged, you offer to close in 30 days. You negotiate a deal at $85,000. You just made $15,000. This is just like the $15,000 you may have worked months to earn at another job. You earned a paper profit of $15,000 without any risk or real upfront money. It happened in the flash of a real estate deal. There are transaction costs and holding costs involved in buying real estate and a real estate commission and taxes to pay when you sell. These expenses will impact your net profit. These will be part of your cost of doing business.

DEAL ONLY IN A SPECIFIC AREA

To make offers and make money, you must research values. Knowledge is the next step. To become an expert at real estate values, you must limit your real estate activities to a specifically defined investment area. This area should contain approximately 25,000 people. If you live in a city, your investment area may be one neighborhood. If you live in a rural area, it can be an entire county. As you will find, real estate agents may not be as knowledgeable about values as you will be for the simple reason that their sales area will usually be much larger than your investment area. Your area may have 5,000 to 10,000 properties. Their areas may have many times as many houses.

Your objective is to become an expert in value in your specific investment area. You should begin to feel confident about your research in two months and you'll probably be one of the few area experts on prices in six months. Knowledge will be your power to make money. Others simply do not have your incentive to learn values.

Real estate is a local business. Prices can vary from one neighborhood to another, from one street to another and from one end of a street to the other. You deal in a small specialized investment area because you must become sensitive to these differences. These differences can spell profit for you. How much does a garage, a basement, a second bathroom, or backyard decks add to a house's value? Is off-street parking or walking to public transportation or proximity to shopping, a highway or a park important? In some areas, each of these variables can be significant. In other areas, they may not significantly affect value. You must know the variables, which ones are important in your area and be able to put a price on them. An extra 1,000 square feet in lot size in the middle of South Dakota may not be significant while 1,000 square feet in the middle of Manhattan may be worth millions. In Manhattan, even the air over a building, called air rights, can be worth millions.

You may find in your area that a garage is worth an extra $10,000, a half bath $5,000, or having a Main Street address $25,000. What about the zoning? What about the lot size? What about the assessment? What about a finished basement? Are there properties with scenic views? What are the variables and what are they worth? This is the research that you are doing. The more you can isolate and identify specific factors affecting property values in your specific area, the more money you'll make.

This system is not just about making low offers on property. It is not simply about seeing a house listed for $150,000 and offering $130,000, although you may make such offers. As you start to work this system, you will begin to find houses listed for less than what they are worth. For example, you may find a $150,000 house listed for $130,000. You could buy the house for the full listed price and still be getting a great deal.

In many parts of the country, there are services, which for a reasonable monthly fee will mail you information on all of the real estate transactions that take place within your investment area. This is public information. You may find the same information recorded at the town hall if you'd like to do the legwork yourself. Increasingly, you will find prior sale information on the Internet. Research may lead you to a great deal of information on property sales including: the names of the buyers and sellers, the sale price, the amount of the mortgage, the name of the lender giving the loan, the lot size, the size of the house, etc.

Research services make the gathering of raw data easy. You'll be able to make databases and charts galore. However, don't be lulled into complacency. To become an expert on real estate values, you've got to get out of your chair and into your car. There is a lot of potential profit at stake. This is not the time to take shortcuts. You can't see beautiful room colors, shoddy construction, a great tiled bathroom, wet basement problems or attic expansion possibilities from a listing sheet or a newspaper ad. Your goal will be to inspect each and every property that comes on the market in your area. Yes, some properties will be out of your price range but you still want to see many of them. Even if your target buys are in the $100,000 to $200,000 price ranges, you still will want to see and understand why some properties sell for $300,000, $400,000 or more. Inspecting properties will become your part-time job. Generally, making an appointment and seeing a property will take less than 30 minutes.

For each property in your investment area, you will want to record the original asking price and the final sale price. What was your initial reaction to the original asking price? You are now the appraiser. Do you feel that the asking price and sale prices were high, low or average? In your opinion, did the new buyer pay too much, get a good deal or an average deal? Most properties sell in 60 days. How long did this property stay on the market? Were you able to glean any special information, such as the size of the downpayment or the name of the lender?

As you go through this fairly simple recording and self-questioning process with each new property on the market, your understanding of values will deepen. At first, you may have few opinions. Later, you will be able readily to differentiate the good buys from the bad deals.

When most residential buyers make offers on property, they are thinking about more than money. They are going to live in the house. They have to like the kitchen and the neighborhood and the schools and local government. When you make offers, you only have to like the price.

When most homeowners are selling property, they are thinking about more than money. They are leaving many memories behind. This house represents their past. They must simultaneously think about leaving and moving to a new kitchen and new neighborhood and new schools. For many people, the home selling process can be quite unpleasant. Many sellers wish to sell as quickly as possible. The seller must keep the house perfect at all times because agents may call at any hour of any day. The entire sales process can be traumatic with strangers of all types milling about the house and a few making rude comments. And consider that you may make an offer of $120,000 for a property that the seller had bought years ago for $20,000. The sellers may be only too happy to take this substantial appreciation and run.

As a novice investor, when you decide to make an offer, don't be intimidated. If your research tells you to offer 20% below the asking price, then hold firm and make this your offer. The agent may balk while the homeowner gladly accepts. You won't know until you make the offer. If the listing term on the house is nearing an end and the agent hasn't sold the house and is in danger

"Now that the children are gone, I'm leasing twenty-seven hundred square feet for immediate occupancy, warehousing several luxury units, and aiming for complete co-op comnversion by early September."

of being replaced, the agent can quickly become your ally.

There are many many reasons why people sell houses. Maybe there has been a death in the family and the survivors want out of the house because of memories. Maybe there is a new baby and a larger house is needed. Maybe there is a new job. Perhaps the owners don't want to do any more maintenance. The owner could have had a fight with the neighbors. Sellers can have many reasons to sell which are not your business or concern. Your single motivation will be price and terms. If you don't get what you want, you move on to the next deal. For you, there will always be a next deal. It is not necessary for you to love a home to profit from it. This is now your business. What happens if the sellers don't like your offer? They can reject it. The sellers are holding the cards and you are not. When it becomes your turn to be the seller, you can decide to accept or reject offers.

HOLDING AND MANAGING INVESTMENT REAL ESTATE

The object of buying and selling property is to make enough money so that you can invest in solid income properties. You will want to make a sufficient downpayment so that the rental income will at least cover your expenses with some surplus. This surplus is called your cash flow. Your cash flow may be small during your early years of ownership and should increase each year, especially if you opt for a fixed rate mortgage.

Many people shy away from the real estate investment business because of a fear of dealing with tenants. However, most successful real estate investors love their tenants. When you buy a property, you will be borrowing many tens of thousands of dollars. You borrow money but you don't really use your own money to pay the loan back. You have these wonderful people called tenants who every month give you the money to pay back your loans. What a great business! You borrow money and someone else pays that money back for you. For example, you might buy a $240,000 six-family apartment building. Your downpayment may be $40,000 and you arrange a $200,000 mortgage for 20 years. Each month, your tenants give you the money to repay your loan. In 20 years, the loan is repaid and you have the $200,000. This is called amortization. In 20 years, the

$240,000 property may be worth $400,000. This is called appreciation. Your $40,000 becomes $400,000. This is not somebody getting lucky and hitting the lottery. This is a typical real estate investment transaction. In every community there are a few people who have figured this out and own the investment real estate. Join them!

Don't be afraid of tenants. Your investment is their home and the vast majority of people treat their homes with the utmost respect. Love your tenants for what they can do for you. They can help make your financial goals a reality.

Managing small investment properties is not particularly difficult or time consuming. If you maintain your properties properly, the time commitment will be in the one hour to two-hour range per property per week. When you have a problem, you react as if you had that problem at home; you call a plumber, electrician or carpenter for help. If you are not skilled yourself, you will be able to find a local general contractor willing to do small jobs.

One of the big advantages to investing in real estate is that you don't have to own much real estate to be wealthy. If you own six small investment properties in your community, you are probably well on your way to an early comfortable retirement. Even one good rental property in addition to your own house can make a significant difference in your retirement.

MISTAKES TO AVOID

This system does not work for everyone for a number of reasons:

1. The geographical area is too large. A smaller area is better than a larger area.

2. The investor becomes impatient. There may be two opportunities in one month and none for four months. Persistence and good research are keys to the system.

3. The research gets stale. The market is constantly changing. Knowledge is power.

4. The investor gets lazy or overconfident. Physically viewing properties and keeping an accurate database of activity is important.

5. The investor lacks confidence. He misses opportunities because of indecision. He is too timid to make offers. Or, he's

pressured by the real estate agent to make offers higher than their research suggests is warranted.

6. The investor gets greedy. She makes unrealistic demands of the agent or seller. She loses a deal with thousands in potential profit waiting for interest rates to drop a fraction. She forever worries about capital gains taxes before they make any capital gains.

7. The investor gets emotional. The investor allows his or her personal preferences for living spaces that he or she aren't going to live in to cloud the financial aspects of the transaction. New owners can make new rules and do any renovations that they choose to do after they acquire the property.

THE HOME REINVESTMENT METHOD

A modified approach to this real estate system is called the home reinvestment method. You search for a good home value. You buy and move into the home. You decorate and improve. You add a hefty profit onto your costs while keeping the property continually on the market. You remain in the house until you sell. You take your profit and find another house. Buying and selling your own house minimizes the holding and security costs of purchasing a vacant house. Holding costs during buying and selling can also be minimized by having a tenant in the property who knows that the property is being marketed. To secure the tenant's cooperation in the marketing process, you may offer them a small percentage of the profit when the property sells.

This chapter is only a mere hint of an idea to motivate you toward self-education in the field of real estate investing. In real estate as in any other business, you want to be informed and stay informed. Keep looking at houses. Keep talking to brokers and other investors. Keep talking to your tenants. Keep reading real estate books. Keep up on prices by reading your Sunday newspaper and local real estate magazines. Keep surfing the Internet for articles and courses on real estate.

There are many other opportunities for real estate profits explained in the *Master Real Estate Course* available on MasterSuccess.com. You can build units. Convert apartments to condos. Split off buildable lots. Finance sales. Become an agent. Form investment partnerships. To further your real estate investment education, you will also want to enroll in the *Master Small Business Course* on MasterSuccess.com. One of the core stories in the *Master Small Business Course* involves a young man starting from scratch who uses the *Master Real Estate Course* to become financially independent.

You can become a real estate investor. There are opportunities to suit most starting budgets and most schedules. You may begin with a small condominium or a large apartment building. If you do your research, you can raise investment capital or make a career out of buying and selling properties. If you own well maintained properties and treat your tenants with respect, with time you should find the real estate investment business to be both lucrative and rewarding.

KEY CONCEPTS

Everyone should invest in real estate. Real estate deals involve tens and hundreds of thousands of dollars. It doesn't take many real estate investments to become financially secure. Small percentage gains when buying or selling add up to large profits. You can control large investments with small percentage down-payments. The object of buying and selling property is to make enough money so that you can invest in solid income properties. You will want the rental income at least to cover your expenses with some surplus.

The most important factor to consider in real estate investing is not location. It is price. Just like any other investment you must buy low and sell high. It is better to buy a $60,000 condo for $40,000 than it is to buy a million-dollar mansion for a million dollars.

In real estate, knowledge is power. Through research it is possible to gain a competitive edge in the marketplace. Real estate is a local business. To become an expert in real estate values, limit your real estate activities to an area containing approximately 25,000 people. In a city, this will be a small neighborhood whereas in the country it might be an entire county. By limiting the area you will be able to learn about every transaction within its boundaries. You'll record the asking and sales prices. You'll observe how long the property was on the market. Then armed with this information you will make offers at a price and on terms where you will profit.

Many people avoid the real estate investment business because they fear dealing with tenants. Real estate investors should love their tenants. You borrow money and your tenants pay that money back for you. In general, managing smaller investment properties requires only about an hour or two per property per week. This is very reasonable when you consider that it only takes owning six small investment properties to have a comfortable retirement.

YOUR ASSIGNMENT

Your assignment for this chapter is to become familiar with real estate values in your area. What is the price range for condos, single-family houses, two-family houses and larger investment properties? Use the Internet, free local real estate magazines or the Sunday newspaper. If you know someone in the real estate business, ask him or her. Knowing prices is the first step. Then you can begin to design a realistic real estate investment program and start to figure out downpayment requirements and financing options. Remember that even if you end up with only your own home and one additional piece of investment property, you will be miles ahead of most people. You will be at the *"A"* level for retirement security.

CHAPTER SEVEN
MASTER HEALTH

I hated every minute of the training, but I said, "Don't quit.
Suffer now and live the rest of your life as a champion."
Muhammad Ali, American boxer (b. 1942)

Your health and safety are everything. If you feel good, you
will be energetic and ready to take on the challenges of successful living. Healthy living habits are forever. Make a personal
commitment to look and feel the best that you've ever looked
and felt. Your smile, your posture, your mannerisms and the
spring in your step will all shout *"Success!"* Your confident manner and awareness will help keep you from harm. There is an
Arabian proverb that states, *"He who has health, has hope; and
he who has hope, has everything."* This chapter will deal with
diet, exercise and self-defense.

By following the Master Success System and the Action
Principles, you will become financially independent. This means
that you will have the extra time and extra resources to travel,
play sports and engage in many recreational activities. You want
to be fit and energized to fully enjoy these activities now and
during all your golden years.

If you want to get in shape, it is important that you confront
the truth that those in the diet/health industry don't want you to
face. Food is comforting and exercise hurts. In the real world,
there often is pain before gain. The word *"pain"* in a health
sense really means discomfort. You aren't subjecting yourself to
serious pain but you probably will become uncomfortable from
dieting and exercise. This is normal and expected. If you can be
honest with yourself and accept that dieting and maintaining
physical fitness takes hard work and a strong commitment, you
can better withstand the lifelong challenges presented by food
and exercise.

When you feel bad or stressed, delicious food can be your

faithful, soothing friend. Eating makes us feel good. Snacking is one of the easiest ways you can spoil yourself. You don't need scientific studies to tell you that chocolate, French fries and ice cream are wonderful mood elevators. Saving for your children's college has a long-term benefit. Eating a blueberry pie has an immediate benefit. You have to be rich to buy a Porsche. Anyone can buy a bacon double cheeseburger. And, eating two donuts in the morning won't have an immediate negative impact on your profile. You can eat a bag of donuts before you reach 3,500 calories and gain a pound.

We love food and food loves us back. Food is a constant temptation that requires strong willpower to resist. Who wants to order a side salad for lunch when the rest of the office has ordered pizza? Willpower. Who doesn't want to eat the fries when we take the kids for fast food? Willpower. Who wants to eat low fat foods that may taste like cardboard? If it were not for the calories, very few people would choose low fat frozen yogurt over high fat ice cream.

You can eat well and sensibly. You probably already know what to do. You already know that broiled, light, fresh, steamed and poached are good words. You already know that fried, stuffed, buttery and au gratin are bad words. You already know that you should eat more fruits and vegetables. You already know that you should be doing healthy things like drinking 8 glasses of water per day, taking a multi-vitamin and for women being sure that your calcium intake is sufficient. Adding a dash of lemon or lime to the water helps. If you feel that you aren't current on proper nutritional theories or advice, go to MasterSuccess.com where you will find links to the best health education sites.

Food is an easy way to challenge yourself, build your self-discipline and feel good about being in control of yourself. You want a candy bar or an ice cream sundae but you fight the temptation. A food craving usually lasts for 15-20 minutes. Wait the 15-20 minutes. Then, you can pat yourself on the back. This is just a little test that you can give yourself. Not eating candy bars and ice cream does not make you a better person. There is nothing wrong with eating an occasional candy bar or ice cream sundae. They are treats and treats are important to our psychic well being. When you do indulge just make sure that you aren't mindlessly shoveling in wasted calories but rather, in the moment, savoring the treat. Are you bored, anxious or really hungry? Eat mindfully.

You know that life provides endless choices. Healthy living is not being 50 and trying to look 20. At any age, healthy living represents vim, vigor and vitality. The more active your lifestyle the stronger will be your ability to ward off feeling old and tired. No one will ever know you better than you know yourself. If you feel that you can and should do more, then do more. Your road to success will involve challenges. You will be faced with choices. One choice will have an immediate benefit. The other choice will be an investment in a better future. Be aware of the choices you make. Seek a balance in your decision making between short-term gratification and long term benefits. However, simply by being aware of the choices that you are making, you will, over your lifetime, tend to make better choices.

Healthy living has to do with many areas besides weight and nutrition. There are many damaging substances and behaviors you must guard against from abusing drugs and alcohol to road rage driving. As such, the anxiety that you may feel as a dieter is not limited to food consumption. These same feelings may be felt and amplified if you try to stop drinking, smoking, taking drugs or even limiting caffeine and driving safely. It will be tough and often physically uncomfortable to eliminate bad habits. You must be tough. There are patches and pills and counseling sessions to help, but in the final analysis, the breaking of long term negative habits will require your inner resolve to be successful.

DIET

Why kid yourself? If you are overweight and you go on a diet, you hurt. It is our obsession with quick fixes that gives us trouble. You can follow any number of popular diets and diet gurus. All of the diet advice about not eating or eating some things and not others probably will work if you are persistent. Eat fewer calories than you expend and the diet works. The problem comes from the cravings. You will be hungry. This is the tough part, the hungry part. When you start to get hungry, your body will tell you that it doesn't like what is happening and you become grumpy, nervous and irritable. Some around you will be less sympathetic with your quest for thinness and will beg you to eat a cupcake and to stop acting like such a jerk. They will give you permission to eat.

You have to prepare yourself for the inevitable negative consequences of the weight losing process. When you want to lash out, you have to stop and take a breath and envision the new you and all the compliments that will inevitably be showered upon you when you become the leaner you. Get in the habit of reading food labels. Eat until you feel full and then stop. In restaurants, order less food or cut your portions in half and take the rest home in a doggy bag. Skip the appetizers and share the desserts. Eating fruits for dessert or snacks is a positive life habit. It takes 10-20 minutes for the food you put in your mouth to reach your stomach and register in your brain so slow down your eating. You may be full sooner than you realize.

The basic rule of thumb of eating: If you are aware of what you are eating 90% of the time, then you don't have to worry about the other 10%. Eat all of the fruits and vegetables you want whenever you want and the odds are overwhelming that you will lose weight and look great.

Safe long-term weight loss involves losing only a pound or two per week. This doesn't sound like much but cumulatively equals 50 to 100 pounds a year. It doesn't have to be too tough. To lose a pound a week, just eat 240 fewer calories a day and exercise enough to burn 300 calories (a brisk 40-minute walk). Keep to the program. Successful entrepreneurs often fail and try again. Successful dieters often fail and try again. Don't give up. Take small steps. Continuously improve. Feel the power of self-control.

Be realistic. There are new diet pills that seem to imply that you can eat all you want and still lose weight. And, from clinical trials and testimonials, there is evidence that the pills work. The pills allow food to bypass the normal digestion process. However, the one little side effect is uncontrollable spontaneous bowel movements. Your willpower, not putting the food in your mouth, may be the more socially acceptable choice.

Dieting is too tough to keep feeling anxious and guilty. You don't want to live a yo-yo life of going on and off diets. If you can, you want to go on one diet and never diet again. You want to set a goal to reach a healthy weight that you can maintain for the rest of your life. You make this decision. If you're a little chunky but this doesn't bother you and you feel energetic, then relax and allow common sense to be your guide. Current research suggests that while being a little bit skinny is pretty good, being a little bit overweight may not be so terrible. It is preferable to be a little bit overweight and fit than to be skinny and unfit. However, 20% of Americans are now classifiable as obese meaning that they are 30 pounds or more overweight. Obesity kills 300,000 Americans each year. Make your choice.

EXERCISE

Just as you've got to be committed to diet and brave your way past harmful addictions, you've got to be committed to keep to a lifelong exercise schedule. Many health problems and diseases can be alleviated through dedication to a daily exercise regime. Being physically fit, you'll live longer, reduce your risk of heart disease and colon cancer, lower or control your blood pressure and help to prevent diabetes while promoting healthy bones, muscles and joints. Working out alleviates feelings of depression and anxiety while promoting psychological well being. There are other incentives to stay active. Most men and women reach their maximum strength levels between ages 20-30. By age 65, individuals who haven't exercised may lose as much as 80% of their youthful strength. In another fifteen years, at age 80, if they are still alive, they may lose another 50% of their strength. The message is clear. You are going to work very hard to have a long and prosperous retirement. Make sure that you are in shape to fully enjoy it.

You do want to eat but you have to do less of it. You don't want to exercise but you have to do more of it. In other words, you have to make time for exercise when you could be doing something better like eating. Exercise can be repetitive and boring. It may

"How long will it be before I feel that I own the night?"

require special equipment or club memberships, both of which cost money. If you are out of shape, you can become discouraged when you try to squeeze into that spandex workout suit. Exercise makes you sweaty and smelly. And, finally, but not least, exercise will hurt you. To get from unfit to fit, prepare yourself for aches and soreness, i.e. discomfort. When you exercise, your body fights back.

Fortunately, our bodies are such physiological marvels, that we don't require much physical conditioning. We just can't abuse our bodies for the ninety plus years they house us. Some people can stay overweight and live long healthy lives. Most can't. Some people can smoke cigarettes and pour in the heavy booze their whole life with little noticeable effect. Most can't. Common sense translated through moderation is your guide. You don't need a lot of food and you don't need a lot of exercise. You just need some of each. This does not mean that living a moderate lifestyle is easy. It isn't. Be strong. Fortunately, by following the Action Principles, you will be strong. Eat less. Exercise more.

Any method you choose to get yourself moving is a good choice. It isn't going to matter a great deal whether you choose to jump rope alone in your apartment or join a fancy health club and work out with a personal trainer. Your muscles won't know the difference. The hardest part of getting to the gym is getting to the gym. Once you are there, your routine should include both cardio and strength work. Your cardio work can be done on the stair machines, ski machines, bicycles or treadmill. Your strength work will involve either using free weights or resistance machines.

You exercise your muscles to the point of fatigue and you feel the effects tomorrow. Tomorrow you go back for more of the same. Plan on exercising three to five days per week. Does this exercise ever end? As a matter of fact, no. It is tough to stick to a regular exercise schedule forever. You do it anyway. You don't expect it to be easy.

THE THREE LEVELS OF FITNESS

There are three basic levels to fitness. Most people aren't even on Level One. They are on Level Zero. They do zero. Seventy-eight percent of adults do not do enough exercise to qualify as preventive health maintenance.

There is Level One, which is the level where people work out to avoid premature death. This is the very basic twenty minutes three times a week of cardio at 60% to 80% of maximum heart rate. Walking on a treadmill or pedaling a stationary bike while watching TV or reading are preferred choices. People on Level One will occasionally think about the stairs instead of the elevator. People at this level may or may not be in good looking shape but nobody's laughing either. If they do look really good, they can probably thank genetics. They are comfortably staying alive.

Level Two people are into fitness. Exercise becomes an important part of the day on four or six days per week. Exercise sessions generally last from forty to sixty minutes. Workouts are planned to include aerobic work for the heart, anaerobic work to build strength and flexibility training to improve range of motion and to help prevent injuries. Level Two people frequently crosstrain between various athletic disciplines and may be competitive in one or more sports. A person who can stay on Level Two, is going to look relatively good as well as feel pretty good.

There is Level Three. Here is an athlete or someone who wants to be known for his or her body. They don't exercise but rather, they train. People on this level can range from serious fitness buffs to those for whom exercise becomes their principle identity. Other aspects of your life may take a backseat to working out. They keep careful and detailed training and performance records. The majority of their friends are "into" the same sport's lifestyle. They may train ten or more hours per week. They probably are being coached. They know all the applicable clubs, magazines and websites for their sports. If you really want to look like a magazine model, plan on Level Three.

If the point is to be healthy, then any of the three levels are acceptable. Moderate exercise or better is the goal. Exercise shouldn't be relegated to the

weekends. Exercise should become a habitual part of your daily routine. On Level One, you are healthy but your physique may not draw comment. On Level Two, you are healthy and look good. On Level Three, you are healthy and are on-call for the magazine cover shoot. The only bad level is Level Zero.

We can all make a decision to try to live to be 90. Babies born in this new millennium may well live to be 100 and beyond. We are all subject to genetics and accidents but we can be in control of most of the rest of what's important about what we eat and whether our activity level is sufficiently high to be considered exercise. There is no such thing as old age when it comes to lifting weights or training to run in a marathon or studying to become a black belt in karate. Get over the excuses. Realize that there are no shortcuts. Realize that healthy living takes some degree of sacrifice and some degree of discomfort. Make healthy living a gift that you give to yourself.

CHOOSE A LIFE SPORT

For all but a few hearty souls, as mentioned, just exercising can become stale. A good way around the tedium is to choose a life sport. A life sport is one that you can enjoy at 9 or 90. Here are a few suggestions:

Archery	Skating	Golf	Tennis	Squash
Swimming	Bowling	Scuba diving	Basketball	
Cycling	Martial Arts	Racquetball	Fishing	Yoga
Running	Aerobics	Boating	Skiing	Walking
Badminton	T'ai chi	Weight lifting	Hiking/climbing	
Aerobic dancing				

What changes can you make in your daily routine to improve your life? If you can feel and look great, why not go for it? Your minimal goal should be to burn 1,000 or more calories per week through exercise. Walking is a good start. Begin your program with daily sessions of about 15 minutes, gradually building up to a half-hour per day. An exercise program doesn't have to be complicated. Here's a simple program: walk 10,000 steps a day. That's it. Get a pedometer and start walking your 10,000 steps.

If you are over 50 or someone at high risk for heart disease you should check with your doctor before significantly increasing your activity level or radically changing your diet. You may find that as the compliments start to roll in and you start feeling younger and younger, healthy living will become one of your best habits.

To become proficient at a sport takes diligent practice. For example, the average person can earn a black belt in karate in three to four years if they take classes and practice an average of three to four times per week. It can be done with patience and perseverance. In learning a new sport, take care to build upon a solid foundation of fundamentals. Slow down and practice your basics. The natural tendency is to want to always seek new material and to rush ahead. This is usually a mistake that frequently leads to early burnout.

Sir Edmund Hillary, the first man to climb Mount Everest, said, *"You don't have to be a fantastic hero to do certain things – to compete. You can be just an ordinary chap, sufficiently motivated to reach challenging goals."* There will be a cold morning when the last thing that you want to do is to get out of a warm bed and exercise. This is a moment of decision. This is the decision that makes all the difference. It's not the nine easy mornings. It's the one tough morning that becomes the bridge between success plateaus. Everyone can or won't make the choice to get up. This is the point. This is why you will succeed. In those moments of decision, you will choose success. And, have fun feeling good and feeling good about yourself. Vince Lombardi, the great American football coach, taught *"Winning is not everything but making the effort is."*

Sir Edmund Hillary

Vince Lombardi

SELF-DEFENSE

To master health, you must become aware of potential dangers to your person. You are responsible for your own protection and to protect those in your care. Awareness is your first best defense. You must train yourself to be aware. Awareness is like any other positive habit. When you enter any room for the first time whether it is a meeting room, hotel room or classroom, you should familiarize yourself with the exits, obstacles that might block exits, crowds, windows, stairs, etc. Awareness is not paranoia. It is common sense self-defense. If you will devote 21 days to conscious practice, awareness will begin to become second nature. Awareness will become automatic.

Awareness will also teach you to notice people and places out of the ordinary. Always follow your instincts. If the people or the surroundings make you feel uneasy, leave and live to enjoy another day. Always know where you are. Wait for the next elevator. Wait for the next taxi. Wait for the next train. If you feel uncomfortable, don't worry about being nice to strangers.

Be familiar with your limitations. Don't think about carrying weapons unless you have been trained to use them properly and you are willing to practice using them both offensively and defensively on a regular basis. This applies to guns, knives, batons, mace, pepper spray or your vehicle. Almost any weapon is better than open hand fighting if you are prepared to make the investment to become a fighter. However, physical confrontation is always a last resort.

If confronted, speak with all the confidence you can muster. Look the person in the eyes, make it short, *"No"* and move on. Let the offender move on to an easier target. If you fight, plan on fighting ferociously and getting hurt badly. The eyes, throat and groin are the best targets. There is no such thing as dirty fighting. You must bite, scratch and kick. Developing fighting skills and a warrior spirit takes years of dedication for a reasonable, sane person who cares about the consequences of his direct actions.

Leaving the scene of trouble is always a better option. Carry a cell phone. Carry and be ready to blow a whistle. Scream *"Fire"* to draw attention to yourself. Make a scene. Carry your keys in your hand and slash and run. Call the police. Call your lawyer. If you are involved in on-going domestic disputes, know the shelters and hot lines that you can contact for help. There is help. You must survive long enough to get that help.

At home, don't open the door if you don't know who is on the other side. If you aren't expecting a serviceman or meter reader, call the office before opening the door. Don't allow strangers into the house. If they have a story about needing to make a phone call, make the call for them without opening the door. Never let anyone on the phone know that you are home alone. Put deadbolts on exterior doors and locks on all windows. If you lose your keys, change the locks. Make sure that hallways, entrances and parking areas are well lit. When vacationing, put your lights and radio on timers. Know your neighbors and have someone pick up the mail or stop delivery. If you come home and suspect a break-in call the police before entering. Program emergency numbers on your home and car and cell phones. Women should be careful about identifying their gender in the phone book, mailbox, on their car, etc. If you are suspicious of anything, go with your instincts and call the police. Don't worry about bothering the police. This is their job to protect you.

If you are out for a walk or run, do it with a partner. Run facing the traffic. Be aware. Know your route. Confine your walk or run to well lit, populated areas. Avoid shortcuts. Don't appear absent-minded. Don't wear headphones. Don't load yourself down with gear and packages. Stay in the middle of the sidewalk. If you are followed, change direction and walk into a store or toward people. Don't get too close to people asking for directions. If uncomfortable, say you don't know. Don't worry about being polite. Never hitchhike. Never get into a car and be driven anywhere. If you are being forced into a car, start fighting for your life right there.

At work, use all of the same precautions. Be aware of safety regulations, procedures and classes. Know the exits and the location of fire alarm boxes. Keep your distance until strangers are properly identified. Don't get on an elevator with anyone with whom you feel uncomfortable. Wait for the next car. Know whom you can go to for help. If you have to work late or have a late class, be sure to arrange to have someone escort you to your car or public transportation. If you are being harassed, you can't change someone else's behavior. Report them if you can or quit if you must.

In your car, always lock the doors. Carry an extra key. Carry your keys in your hand when approaching the car. In a parking garage, only give the attendant your car keys and not all your keys. Look around and in your car before entering. If suspicious, call the police or security on your cell phone. A well maintained car is your responsibility. Keep the tank at least half full at all times. Each year, over 3,000 people are killed making roadside repairs. If you break down, stay in the car and phone for help. Do not open the door or window to strangers. Always carry enough cash or credit to take a taxi or other transportation home. If you are followed, drive to a police station, fire station or other populated spot and start honking the horn until help arrives.

When taking public transportation, sit in an occupied car near the driver. If your instincts tell you to move, move. If you are being bothered, report the incident. If you are being followed, do not get off at your regular stop. Go to a crowded place and mingle. Seek help if necessary. Keep baggage to a minimum. Stay alert and do not wear headphones. If you are in a taxi or bus, make sure that the driver's picture matches the picture on the license. If not, get out. There are lots of potential victims. Again, if you appear confident, the offender will probably wait for a better target.

The chances are overwhelming that the biggest threat to you is yourself. Protect yourself from yourself. One of the Action principles asks you to Heed The Warnings. This means be smart. Wear seat belts. Don't drive in a car with anyone who thinks that it's OK to have a few drinks and drive or that it's OK to drive at high speeds. If a boat is too crowded, don't get on. If a party is too crowded, leave. If the weather is bad and you have the option of not flying, don't fly. Be smart. Be aware. Heed the warnings. Save yourself.

If you are interested in learning more common sense self-defense tips, go to our companion martial arts and peace website at Dojo.com or take the *Master Self-Defense Course* at MasterSuccess.com.

KEY CONCEPTS

To master health you must control yourself. You must have the self-discipline to continue your diet and exercise program in the face of discomfort. The diet industry tries to sell people on the idea that they can eat all they want and lose weight. Diet gurus try and sell you quick fixes. This is nonsense. You must make a lifetime commitment to your diet and fitness.

To succeed you must be prepared for the hard work that will be necessary. You need to read food labels and pay attention to how much you are eating. When you are full stop eating. It takes 20 minutes for your appetite to subside after you eat. Remember this and slow down eating.

You should aim to lose a pound or two each week. This

sounds like very little but it is 50-100 pounds in a year! If you cut 240 calories a day from your eating and add 300 calories a day in exercise you can lose a pound a week. If you are older you should check with your doctor before starting an exercise program or seriously changing your diet.

You should adopt an active lifestyle. Choose an exercise that you will stick with. Start slowly if you have to but start. Plan on exercising three to five days a week. Perform cardiovascular exercises to burn calories and improve your resistance to heart disease and use free weights or resistance machines to build strength. Choose a life sport – a physical activity that interests you that you can enjoy for a lifetime.

Being fit and healthy is really very simple; begin eating healthy foods and exercising and keep doing it for the rest of your life.

Practice common sense self-defense. Learn to be aware and to follow your instincts. Avoid fighting but if you have to fight make sure that it is for your life and that you fight accordingly.

YOUR ASSIGNMENT

Your assignment for this chapter is to go to the MasterSuccess.com website and find your recommended weight range. Then write down your plan for reaching this weight by a specific date. Also commit to an exercise program of at least three times per week. Next, go to Dojo.com and see if the philosophy behind the martial arts can help you in your quest for healthy living. Practice awareness for the next 21 days. Finally, choose or investigate a life sport in which you have a personal interest.

CHAPTER EIGHT
MASTER MIND

We are what we think. All that we are arises with our thoughts.
With our thoughts, we make our world.
Gautama Buddha, Indian religious philosopher (b. 563 BC)

Good mental health is a gift that you give yourself. To maintain good mental health, you must start with good mental health. It is living in reality. You must have a reasonably well thought through concept of the meaning of your life. You must have a strong character built on a foundation of core beliefs that guide your daily life. Perhaps, as a youngster, you were exposed to positive values at home, at school, at church or from youth sports or scouting. At any time, anyone can benefit from the guidance of the *Bible*, *Talmud* or *Koran*. You can embrace the Ten Commandments, the Beatitudes, the American Bill of Rights and the Constitution. You can read the classics. You can follow other positive guidelines, such as the Action Principles. You can become the master of your moods. You can't always control what happens to you, but you can control what happens inside you.

Happiness is a state that you can choose right now. Over two

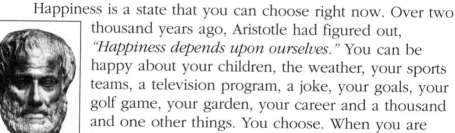
Aristotle

thousand years ago, Aristotle had figured out, *"Happiness depends upon ourselves."* You can be happy about your children, the weather, your sports teams, a television program, a joke, your goals, your golf game, your garden, your career and a thousand and one other things. You choose. When you are happy, you are successful. Make sure that you have created a strong link between success and happiness. When you reach your goals, you don't want to be greedy and smug, you'll want to feel fulfilled and happy.

From a base of good mental health, you must take time every day to rest, relax and recharge. You invest this time to make the minor adjustments that keep your life balanced. You invest this time to develop and maintain the style and the attitudes of an achiever ready to stay the course. Through relaxation and meditation, you become calm yet invigorated. Relaxing allows you to wash away the mental muddle of your busy days. Reflection will give you the opportunity to separate fact and truth from rumor and conjecture. Five hundred years before the birth of Christ, the Indian religious philosopher Gautama Buddha was preaching, *"Learn to let go. That is the key to happiness."* You build the strength necessary to admit your mistakes, forgive others and move on. You will feel renewed. Peace and tranquillity through quiet time will become your private refuge. You will cherish this time that you spend with yourself.

BUILD YOUR SELF-CONFIDENCE

Over the long term, good mental health resulting from personal introspection will help you to develop an inner character that you will be proud to show and share with the world. It will also help you deal with human conditions and situations that develop beyond your control. You must feel comfortable with yourself and with the decisions you make. Some of your decisions will demand serious contemplation and may involve a dubious payoff years in the future. This is where self-confidence becomes so important. There are no guarantees. Reflecting upon what you have done, why you took the actions you did and how you will act in the future will all combine to build your self-confidence.

Remember that just as most people aren't exercising enough, aren't watching their diets, aren't organizing their days with to-do lists, and aren't investing, aren't taking advantage of opportunities, they aren't taking time each day for daily reflection. Why will you succeed when others fail? You will be a person of action doing what others can't or choose not to do. This includes investing in your mental health through solitary reflection. You are the visionary who must see your own bright future.

CONCENTRATE ON THE GOOD

If your posture and your attitude exude confidence, you will not only feel good, you will look good. You will live a high quality life. You aren't naïve believing the world and everything in it to be perfect. Yet you believe that people tend to find what they are looking for. If you concentrate on the bad and what doesn't work and what isn't beautiful and how everything isn't quite to your liking that's what you'll find. If you concentrate on the good, you will find much more to smile about. It is a conscious choice to view your world as pleasant. You can choose to see the good in people. It is a conscious choice to see the good in others. This is what it means to have a positive mental attitude. Be hopeful. St. Jerome preached, *"Begin to be now what you will be hereafter."*

HOW WILL YOU REACT TO CHALLENGES?

You are the person responsible for saving yourself from the mounting stresses associated with daily living. You are the one who has to rebound from the inevitable mistakes and disappointments associated with being a person of action. To be successful, you must move beyond the comfort of the status quo and risk. As you move through the learning curve toward the better you, at times you may feel that you have every right to feel discouraged. You will feel that you should have listened to those who advised caution or inaction. It will be tough to maintain a positive mental attitude in spite of the setbacks and the occasional *"I told you so."* These are the important moments of decision. It's when you hear the criticism or when you realize that you have made a big mistake. It's when you have to admit that a lot of time, talent and money may have been wasted. Will you choose to quit or bounce back? It is how you decide to react in these challenging defining moments that ultimately will make all the difference. Stick to it. Twenty three hundred years ago, Aristotle was teaching his students, *"Criticism is something we can avoid easily – by saying nothing, doing nothing, and being nothing."* This was mentioned in the chapter on Mastering Work. Even if you can get away with it, do you really want to be a pathetic little person forever hiding in the background while others take the risks and do the hard work?

You are the one who must decide to become tough enough to withstand the consequences of mistakes, failures and cynicism. You are the one who must step forward and say, *"Don't worry. I'll do it."* You are the one who must decide to be kind enough to treat others as you wish to be treated even when the reverse doesn't happen. You are the one who must decide to dare to risk in pursuing a course of action leading to wealth. You are the one who has to deal with the daily annoyances of the rude and indifferent behavior of others.

You act when it is time to act. You stay out of it when it is none of your business. You know the difference. You do this for yourself. You teach this to your children. You are the one who has to have the patience and firm resolve to raise responsible children. It is not the movies, television, their friends or their teachers. It is you and them. You do not abdicate but rather accept responsibility for your children. You know what is right. Stand firm. Be patient. Make this investment in their early years and later rest assured. The well being of children is so important to a parent's mental health that this topic will be covered in more depth in the next chapter, Master Relationships. Some parents will raise children who will be self-reliant adults by age 20. Some parents will be living with adult age children for the rest of their lives.

You must also have the inner fortitude and peace of mind to deal with the accidents and misfortunes that are outside of your control: a sick child, loss of a parent, a plant closing, abandonment or rejection by a loved one, crime, personal illnesses or natural disasters. Things may happen that are so devastating that you can't rationally put them into perspective. You can only put your faith in God's grand plan. Be accepting. You can only do the best you can. In the 3rd century before Christ, Aristotle said, *"The ideal man bears the accidents of life with dignity and grace, making the best of the circumstance."*

MATERIAL SUCCESS OFTEN MEANS NOTHING

What happens if you are hard charging and don't take time to consider the consequences of your actions? Success means nothing if you are a professional athlete hooked on drugs. Success means nothing if you are a corporate executive who abuses his family. Success means nothing if you achieve great things and yet have no pride in their accomplishment. Success means nothing if you have to lie, cheat or steal your way to win an advantage.

Good mental health demands that you be honest with yourself. No one else is looking. This is you. Because there are major events in our lives that we can't control, we must become more self-disciplined to control in a positive way all that is within our power to choose. Your mental health depends on it. Two drinks is not ten drinks. Driving 65 is not driving 85. Spending one night out with friends is not four nights. Buying one new pair of shoes is not buying three pairs. Watching an hour of television is not watching all night every night. Giving a few dollars every once in a while to charity is not giving back what you really can. Gambling ten dollars is not risking half your paycheck. Control yourself or admit that you need help and get it. Your journey is only over when God calls you and until then you can pick yourself up and keep moving forward. If you have done wrong to others, you can try to make amends. Realize that others may be under no moral obligation to forgive you. In most cases, your sincerity will win you another chance. In rare instances, man will not or can not forgive and only God can forgive.

YOU NEED TIME OFF

You'll need 20-30 minutes per day of quiet time. You need seven to eight hours of sleep every night. You need at least one day off per week. Consider treating yourself and family to a

mini-weekend vacation every month. Two weeks of annual vacation is a good idea. Off time gives you time to put your life in perspective. Plan your individual and family relaxation time and guard this time as jealously as any of your other activities. Let the phone ring. Let the mail pile up. Relax and enjoy.

Successful people are thoughtful. You decide what you want and why you want it. You test your ideas and conclusions during your quiet time. When you make a mistake, your quiet time will allow you to consider calmly your options and the next best course of action. You thought about it. You tried. You were wrong. You learned. Next. You interpret life's events with emotional maturity. Being a thoughtful relaxed person of action, if you are persistent, the odds favor your eventual success.

Quiet reflection will make you a stronger communicator in that you will have planned your comments in advance. You will be more focused and concise. You will have time to logically reason through options making you better at conflict resolution and negotiation. You should become more patient and be better able to differentiate between what you can change and what you must accept as beyond your ability to change. You will allow yourself the opportunity to replace negative thoughts, prejudices and positions with positive ones. President Thomas Jefferson said, *"Nothing can stop the man with the right mental attitude from achieving his goal. Nothing on earth can help the man with the wrong mental attitude."*

Thomas Jefferson

ACCEPTING DAILY LIFE

In speaking of the joy of loving, helping and caring for others as you build positive relationships, you realize that your good intentions may not be reciprocated. You are not naïve. You fully realize that there are bad people in the world. There are lazy, boorish, stupid, perverted, mean and inconsiderate people. God gave man free will. Some don't do very well with this freedom. Some people act badly in moments of decision. Some people act badly almost all the time. As you master success and begin to travel the world, you will find that the overwhelming majority of people from all cultures and all countries are just like you with the same aspirations to lead prosperous and peaceful lives. The overwhelming majority anywhere will welcome your hand extended in friendship. Yet, awareness teaches us that some groups must be watched and some individuals must be guarded against.

Do all you can for those who can't help themselves. However, you are under no obligation to serve those who could do for themselves and instead choose to be mean or selfish. The people who voluntarily work with mean and selfish people are called saints. Being your best does not obligate you to seek canonization. You can't impose your will on others. You can only encourage good behavior as you set a positive personal example. You can make the personal choice to be positive as you brush aside the minor daily annoyances that everyone faces. You resist the temptation to compound the time given to petty problems by relating your travails to others.

On occasion, letting the moment pass is difficult. You may feel slighted or indignant. You may feel that you have every right to strike back. Discipline yourself to remain silent when you are angry. This isn't easy for anyone. Anger saps your energy and can cloud your reasoning. Find a way around it. Wait. Breathe. Consider. This is self-control. Do your best.

You are cut off in traffic. The incident is already over before you can react. Why upset yourself? The offender is gone. Do you want your success in life to be judged by how many cars you can pass until you lose your license, are in an accident or swerve in front of someone even crazier than you? You can choose to play road rage and *"follow the loser"* or you can choose to get back to enjoying your favorite CD as the incident passes.

Your medium steak is delivered well done. You can eat the steak. You can wait for a new steak to be re-cooked. These are your only choices. You can not undo the past. Get upset and ruin the meal for everyone or relax and enjoy your wine while the staff corrects the problem.

The queue at the Registry of Motor Vehicles is thirty minutes long. This line was not formed just to annoy you. Take out your book and wait your turn.

You are experiencing everyday life. Be patient. Others notice those in control.

Look at the motive of your offender. Most angry, negative people are not out to get you. The road-rager has no idea who you are. Neither does the chef nor the Registry clerk. They are wild, mad and upset. Let them be. They are ruining their lives. Don't let them affect your moment. Don't argue in haste. Consider your options after a good night's sleep.

LIFE TEACHES THE MASTER

Many people find it difficult to accept criticism and will immediately assume a defensive pose waiting to counterattack. They only listen to hear for an opening so that they can strike back. They learn nothing. Can you reverse this thinking? Someone treats you in an inconsiderate way. You can get angry and strike back. Or, you can look at the incident as an opportunity to train your will and skill. Go with the force. When you are pushed, pull. When you are pulled, push. You can go further and in your mind you can thank the offender for presenting you with this opportunity to be the master of your emotions. To be mentally strong, you must practice and pass many of these small tests. It is not easy. It is the journey.

Of course, being human and imperfect, you accept that a critical evaluation of your efforts may be justified. Listen for constructive criticism. You may learn of mistakes that you can correct. You may learn of important steps that you may have skipped. You may learn of alternative strategies, perspectives, ideas and theories. You may be introduced to new successful models to copy. You may identify new resources or personnel who could assist your work. In any of these cases, criticism may be disguised as an opportunity for improvement. Life is teaching you a lesson if you pay attention.

You must be equally on guard against false praise. The well-meaning flattery of others may lull you into the belief that you can stop learning and practicing. You will never learn so much that you can't learn more. You will never wish to stop growing. You are not easily tricked. Be the master.

There are times to intercede, render an opinion or defend. And, there are other times when if a situation hasn't got anything to do with you, be quiet and stay out of it. Often, with reflection, you will see that it may be best to stick to your priorities and let others solve their own problems. Again, you can't change others. You can only live as an example for oth-

"Are we there yet?"

ers who choose to see.

You do not want to live a life where your happiness only comes from special events; birthdays, anniversaries, holidays, vacations or Saturday nights out. On your journey, you want to feel happy as you take each step throughout each day knowing that you are doing your best to both work and relax at your personal master level. You are doing this for yourself, those you love and those who are your responsibility. You are proud. You are calm. You are happy.

HOW TO MEDITATE AND RELAX

Meditation is a practice that leads to spiritual enlightenment and is encouraged in many different religions: Buddhism, Islam, Hinduism and Christianity. In silent meditation, you often feel the link between you and a higher power. You will hear your inner self. Find yourself in the words of the Chinese philosopher Lao-Tzu, *"He who knows others is wise. He who knows himself is enlightened."*

In the Master Success System, meditation can be done in a variety of ways. Meditation can be sitting cross-legged on a pillow in an incense filled room saying mantras "Hmmm ..." or chanting. But, meditation can also be praying, gardening, taking a hot shower, stretching, yoga, t'ai chi, or going for a walk. If you choose an active form of meditation, you want the physical motions to be mindless. You want to minimize the possibility of interruption. Go to a quiet place, a regular place. You want to be alone with your thoughts. Be silent, breathe and relax. This is meditation. It is breathing in and breathing out. It is being conscious of your actions. Awareness. Pay attention as you wash the dishes. Listen to your breathing. Quiet your mind.

Look for opportunities to concentrate on the now. Be consciously aware and mindful. Meditation brings you to the present moment. Taste the food as you eat it. Feel the wind in your face as you run. Feel the muscles as you exercise. Feel the sweat. Feel all of life. Meditation should leave you feeling invigorated and awakened. Some like to slow themselves to the sound of a bell or gong ring. The term *"Buddha"* means *"the awakened one."* Smile.

Meditation can certainly help you on your path to self-discovery. The self-discovery you seek, however, should not be an egotistical exercise where you look for individual characteristics that make you great. Your self-discovery should result in your finding the bonds that link you with all other humans. As was just said, you are remarkably like everybody else. As you make this personal discovery, you will know how your words can hurt or soothe, your touch can injure or reassure, your example can destroy or inspire. The master walks that middle line and is neither overly influenced by criticism nor praise.

Relaxing is even easier and less formal. You can relax at any time. You can relax for ten minutes or one minute. Sit comfortably and close your eyes. Inhale through your nose and count to 6. Slowly exhale through your mouth as you count down from 6. Repeat for several minutes. Concentrate on your breathing with longer and deeper inhales and exhales. Practice breathing from your center, which is just below your navel. Control the flow of your breath without straining. Feel your belly rather than your chest rise and fall. Deep and long breathing is associated with calmness while weak and shallow breathing is associated with anxiety. You want to be as serene as possible without falling asleep. When worries appear, let them float by like floating clouds or see them disappear as a pebble slowly falling to the bottom of a pond. Relax. Tense and release the muscles in your body. Start with the toes. Tense the muscles for a few seconds and release. Go to the calves, thighs, abs, pecs, back, fingers, hands, lower arms, upper arms, neck and finally the muscles in the face. Feel warm and relaxed.

When difficulties arise, bring your mind back to your breathing in and out. Before any stressful situation, breathe through your nose filling your lungs as your stomach rises. Loosen the muscles in your face. Loosen your jaw. Let your shoulders hang. Relax your hands as if you were holding a baby chick. Your body will slow, allowing you to concentrate on the task at hand. Relax and bring yourself back to center.

Focus on all the positive energy that surrounds you. There are lots of people who want to see you succeed. You are a good person. You will be a good parent, friend and boss. Focus your energy on your ability to do good. Relax. Control your breathing and your posture. If you meditate regularly, it will touch all areas of your life. As you learn to control your breathing and relax, you will feel the power of your spirit grow. You will learn a lot about a wonderful person – you! You are the Master Piece.

How to Solve Your Personal Problems

Mentally healthy people aren't people without problems but people willing to confront and deal with the problems they have. What are you anxious about? What are you worried about and what's the worst that can happen? Will the problem definitely occur or is it only a possibility? How serious is the problem? Can you deal with it yourself or should you call for the help of others? Is worrying about the problem worse than the problem? Is there a simple or immediate solution? How would a coward act? How would one of your heroes respond? Have you successfully resolved a similar problem in the past? Now, how will the self-confident and capable you handle this problem? As you consider your options, remember the French proverb, *"One may go a long way after one is tired."* You are tired. You want to do anything else but deal with this problem. You deal with it anyway. It is resolved. You move on.

Quiet time is very important to problem solving. It helps you to focus on the matter at hand, eliminate extraneous points and develop workable solutions and options. And, perhaps, most importantly, it allows you to clarify if the problem under discussion is the actual problem or just a convenient or socially acceptable substitute for a deeper hidden concern. Make sure that the problem you are solving is the real problem.

- Begin by precisely defining the problem. Stick to the issue.
- Analyze the problem from different perspectives.
- Consider solutions. If appropriate, brainstorm with others or seek professional help.
- Consider the ramifications of different solutions.
- Choose your best option.
- Take action.
- Follow - up. Review. Adjust.
- Move on.

How to pray

Faith enriches your life. Belief in God is a wonderful blessing. You will have an anchor to secure your life. You will have a solid values base upon which to build your plans. You will have a guide to govern your business and personal life. You will have comfort in times of need. You will have thoughtful clergy from whom to seek counsel. You will have an ally in raising responsible children. You will have a place to meet nice friends. It isn't easy to go to church or synagogue or the mosque every week or to follow the tenets of the *Bible, Talmud* or *Koran.* That's why a faith in God translated into everyday life can become such an integral part of your success system. It takes some effort but the rewards of the effort are extraordinary.

With humility, submit. Every religion has prayers. A prayer is your conversation with God. Your success and happiness is God's loving answer. Listen for God's messages and instructions. Your selfless good works in helping others are your prayers put into action. The theologian Teilhard de Chardin gave perspective to life with his message, *"We are not human beings having a spiritual experience. We are spiritual beings having a human experience."*

Teilhard de Chardin

William James, the 19th century American philosopher observed, *"If you act a certain way long enough, it becomes you. When you act loving a funny thing happens. You start to feel loving."*

Hold your tongue. Give the homeless man a dollar. Don't spread the gossip. Allow those in a rush to rush by. Do a good job at work. Study. Work on eliminating a bad habit. Smile. Give thanks. You are saying a prayer. Choose to live within this state of grace. God notices.

If you want to experience the power of prayer, you might want to recite Michelangelo's favorite prayer, *"Lord, grant that I might always desire more than I can accomplish."* A trip to Florence, Italy will confirm that God blessed Michelangelo and through him gave priceless gifts to the world.

William James

Choose a prayer book from your religion and choose a daily passage to ponder. Choose a quote from one of the *Positive Mental Attitude* books and consider the author's intent in terms of your own life.

HOW TO CLEAR THE SLATE

Clear the slate. Every day is a new day. Any moment can be an important moment of decision that changes everything.

Would it be helpful to you to keep a journal or diary of your thoughts? Whatever has been bothering or pleasing you, write it down. Some find it helpful to keep the writings as a reference. Others find it cathartic to *"get it off their chest"* and tear up or burn the bad thoughts or mistakes. Keep trying but don't be too hard on yourself. You aren't a loser or an idiot because you made a mistake. Don't beat yourself up. Be kind to yourself. The path on your journey was never going to be perfectly smooth. Now that you know better and are more experienced, move on. If you are persistent, you will make progress.

Roman Catholics have the sacrament of reconciliation to

Mother Teresa

address the past and begin again with hope. Mother Teresa taught, *"It is by forgiving that one is forgiven."* Clergy from all religions are trained as counselors to offer solace, comfort and advice. Every community has mental health professionals from psychologists to marriage counselors offering support groups and individual therapy. Talk to your parents, teachers and friends. If you need help, don't procrastinate and make the problem worse. Take action. Whatever your problem, there are responsible people who will help you. If you don't like one person's ideas, ask another. If different people give you the same answer, you'd better listen. Help yourself.

Be a friend. If you are close to someone who may benefit from professional mental health care, take the risk and tell him or her. Don't give up on them. Use that persistence. Help others. Anne Frank, the brave little girl who was a victim of the Holocaust, lives on in the power of her message, *"How wonderful it is that nobody need wait a single moment before starting to improve the world."*

Consider how people who have had near death experiences talk about reappraising their lives. There seems to be a soul cleaning that takes place after being given a second chance at life. All of a sudden big problems and concerns don't seem that big. All of a sudden little things like smiles and kind words and birds singing and sunsets become important. They may speak of their lives having new purpose and of living to enjoy every precious minute of life. You don't have to wait until you are on your deathbed to look back and wonder *"What if?"* You can start appreciating and living your life now.

Anne Fronk

HOW TO USE VISUALIZATION

Can you see yourself being handed the diploma, breaking the tape at the finish line, and hearing the applause in your honor?

Visualize. Close your eyes. See the new you in your entire splendor. What you can see in your mind can be your guide to attainment. See it. See it every day. Do it. Do it every day. This is your movie. You are the star. You are an actor playing yourself. Fake it as you make it. The stronger your visualized impressions, the more the odds for attainment turn in your favor. Visualization is internal practice. You replace practicing with your body with practicing with your mind.

Visualize now and later. See yourself at your best right now. Right now, the only thing that stands between you and your goals is a little bit of time. See yourself after a month and after six months and after a year of hard work and commitment to your goals.

Peak performance starts in the mind. Many athletes use visualization to picture themselves performing at their best. They learn to concentrate through visualization. They learn to train in their minds even when they can't physically practice. You can do the same. See yourself in a year, five years, in your golden years. See yourself enjoying the full fruits of your labor. You will be successful. You will have both peace and prosperity. See it all. Try to involve all of your senses in the imaging: see, hear, taste, feel, and smell. As you immerse yourself in your future, ideas for how to get there will start to emerge. Put yourself in your best performance mode. Believe. The ways will come.

Who is the person with whom you are most comfortable? What is the one place where you are most comfortable? What was the scene of your greatest achievement? Immerse yourself. Be there.

Go to a relaxing spot in your mind. Breathe deeply. Concentrate on the details of your accomplishments. See the cars, the house, and the clothes. See the respect in the people's eyes that you have helped. Touch the fine fabric of your suit. Taste the wine. Feel the handshake. Use your senses to help your imagination complete this wonderful scene.

Mother Teresa used visualization in her work when she described seeing Jesus in every face. Often questioned about the difficulty of her work with the poor and the sick, she would comment on how many clever disguises Jesus had. Every day, Mother radiated proof that you see in life what you choose to see. You choose. Your mind can only hold one thought at a time. Why not make that thought a positive one?

How to simplify your life

Do you need a $100,000 college education or a $40,000 car or a $300,000 house? If you can, go to a state college, drive a less fancy car or live in a smaller house. If you can do with less, you give yourself a gift of many more favorable options.

In the Master Success System, the idea of life simplification is important. Life simplification is not driving a junk car, eating seeds and wearing dirty clothes that smell like a wood stove. Instead, simplification is living a life with a purpose. From your goal setting and time management, you know what is important to you and design your life around these goals, objectives, values and interests. If you really like restoring antique cars, fishing with your grandchildren, making quilts with your girlfriends or playing the guitar with a local band, you should find ways to do more of what you love and you work to pare away the rest.

Every day, you'll know how to make the correct personal choices for you and no one else. Every day, decision by decision, you mold your future for good or bad. You can simplify your life and have more time and money for your dreams or complicate and clutter your life with more draining activities.

Quiet time helps you get rid of mental junk. Now, get rid of the physical clutter that you don't need. If you haven't worn it or used it in a year, give it to charity.

Guiding Lights

Are you trapped by someone else's negative thinking? Are you victim to someone else's anger, envy, loneliness, mistakes, phobias, depression, prejudices, idiosyncrasies or weaknesses? Are you victim to someone else's goals, dreams, priorities, politics or values?

We live in a wonderful era when the greatest teachers can enter our lives conveniently through books, audiotapes, video and the Internet. The messages of the world's great religious leaders are truly non-denominational and speak to anyone who will stop to listen.

At MasterSuccess.com and our companion website Dojo.com, you will find many links to peace and serenity. The current works or legacies of any of these people, among many others, can help you bring balance to your life: Rabbi Harold Kushner, Mother Angelica, Father Benedict Groeschel, Pope John Paul II, Billy Graham, Robert Schuller, Jesse Jackson, the Dalai Lama or Tich Nhat Hanh. Their words and ideas are a loving gift to you. It was Gandhi who said, *"The difference between what we do and what we are capable of doing would solve most of the world's problems."*

Gandhi

KEY CONCEPTS

You need at least one day off per week. You need 20-30 minutes each day of quiet time. You test your ideas during this time. You make decisions. You consider calmly your options in the face of mistakes and setbacks.

Learn to relax and simplify your life. Clear your mind. Release the stress. Relax. You can relax by sitting comfortably, closing your eyes and slowing your breathing. Deep and long breathing brings peace and calmness. You can relax at any time. You can relax for ten minutes or one minute.

Practice meditation. Go to a quiet place, a regular place. You want to be alone with your thoughts. Be silent, breathe and relax. This is meditation. It is breathing in and breathing out. It is being conscious of your actions. Listen to your breathing. Be consciously aware and mindful. Meditation brings you to the present moment.

Visualize your future. Close your eyes. What you can see in your mind can be your guide to attainment. See it every day. Do it every day. The stronger your visualized impressions, the more the odds for attainment turn in your favor. Visualization is internal practice. Peak performance starts in the mind.

YOUR ASSIGNMENT

Your assignment for this chapter is to commit to a period of quiet time each day for the next 21 days. Allot 20 – 30 minutes. Decide how and where and when you would like to spend that time meditating and relaxing. Consciously be alone with yourself in the moment and see so much.

CHAPTER NINE
MASTER RELATIONSHIPS

To laugh often and much; to win the respect of intelligent people and affection of children; to earn the appreciation of honest critics and endure the betrayal of false friends; to appreciate beauty, to find the best in others; to leave the world a bit better, whether by a healthy child, a garden patch or a redeemed social condition; to know even one life has breathed easier because you have lived. This is to have succeeded.
Ralph Waldo Emerson, American writer (b. 1803)

If you have completed the chapter assignments and have begun to integrate the Action Principles into your personal life philosophy, you are well on your way to mastering success. The simple changes and adjustments that you are making in your attitudes and actions are beginning to reward you with the pride and power of accomplishment. You can see a better life. This will not be a solitary life lived as a monk in a mountain cave. You have chosen a rich, full, rewarding, action packed life filled with people. Everything you need, people around you can give you: love, money, respect, companionship, fulfillment and the reasons to challenge yourself to be your best. Your personal relationships then become very important. Be prepared. Controlling and developing your personal relationships to a master's level will take your emotional intelligence, your patience and your selflessness.

Personal relationships are more important than money or things. A happy marriage and a happy family are worth everything. Pope John Paul II teaches, *"The family is the basic cell of society. It is the cradle of life and love, the place in which the individual is born and grows. Mankind's future is determined in the family."*

Pope John Paul II

To prepare yourself to master your relationships, you must humbly accept your limited ability to change others. Instead, you stand to gain much more by being empathetic or trying to see things through others' eyes. What do your husband, wife, children, employees or customers want? What are their goals? Are you helping or hindering them? Don't guess or presume. Ask them. The easiest way to bond with a person is to focus on their wants and needs. Do what they want or listen for clues that can lead to compromise.

Try this little experiment. During your quiet time today, imagine that you were told that you only had one more day to live. How would you prepare yourself? What would you try to accomplish? Who would you try to meet? What would you say to them? With whom would you like to make amends? The follow-up to this experiment will be discussed at the end of this chapter.

COMMUNICATION IS THE KEY

To have an effective conversation you have to be willing to listen. Follow Socrates' advice and listen twice as often as you talk. Use two ears and one mouth. The word communication comes from the Latin word *"cumminico"* meaning *"to share."* Pay attention. Be aware of body language. Give and expect respect. Be open and flexible. Don't wait for the other party to be positive. Be positive first. Be unafraid of the consequences of truth, sincerity and honesty.

You must work to create an environment for relationship building. Regardless of individual commitments, families should find opportunities for everyone to be together for home cooked meals at least several times per week. For families with school age children, the goal should be for the children to eat with one or both parents every day. This should be considered quality family time. Positive conversation should be stressed. There should be no moaning, complaining or rushing to be excused. Rules for good manners and mutual respect should be mandated. The telephone answering machine should be on and the television off. No books, headphones or video game players are allowed. This family bonding should be extended to outings and vacations. The message should be loud and clear, *"We care about you and what you have to say."*

How you relate to other people does not usually change with

circumstance. Just as family cohesiveness and relations are taken seriously at home, the same team building should be a priority at work. Managers should set up formal and informal meeting opportunities. The boss doesn't always have to act like the boss. Creative suggestions should be encouraged and rewarded. Constructive criticisms should be acknowledged and problems dealt with when they are small. Employees should feel both appreciated and an integral part of the whole. The importance of customer relations in building loyalty should be stressed.

As a member of the Master Success System, be prepared to take the lead. An *"I love you"* to a family member, a *"Nice job"* to an employee and a *"Thank you"* to a customer can go a long

way toward building and maintaining solid relationships. At home, a single rose, a handwritten note, an unexpected toy can bond. At work, a raise or bonus or day off can make an employee feel wanted. To a customer, an extra service or a special price can create a positive relationship conducive to repeat business. This would please Mother Teresa who said, *"Kind words can be short and easy to speak, but their echoes are truly endless."*

Mother Teresa

When Communication Fails

Still, in the real world, small gestures and platitudes may not always be enough. You are always dealing with individuals with individual agendas beyond your control. A family member may engage in destructive behavior. An employee may demand wages and benefits beyond your ability to comply. Some customers can not be satisfied. Keeping lines of communication continually open at least gives you the opportunity for early intervention. On rare occasions, even with patience and reason, all you may be able to do is to restate your position, set limits, and outline possible consequences. Finally, you may have no recourse except to back off. Your forceful persuasion may be elegant and cathartic to you but will probably do little to change someone who is unmotivated to change himself or herself.

Broken marriages, alienated children, lost friends and failed business deals can often be traced back to poor communication. Somebody wasn't listening to what somebody else was saying. If your listener is lazy, distracted, disinterested or absorbed by his or her own side issues, little effective communication is likely to take place. Likewise, if your arguments are seen as false, disorganized or prejudiced, they will tend to fall on deaf ears. There are those who actively seek to listen and learn. There are those who are self-absorbed and want to hear nothing. There are those who pretend sincerity but inside they are actually dismissive of your advice. You can only let them know that if and when they are ready to commit to constructive dialogue that you are always ready to talk reasonably and seek compromises that do not infringe on your values.

You will listen. You will try to help. You will promote reconciliation. You will make reasonable accommodations to their personal likes and dislikes. You will repeat how interested you are in a sound relationship in which all parties benefit and no one is injured. If you are wrong, you will admit it immediately and ask for forgiveness. If you are wronged, you will do your best to forgive and forget quickly.

The long-term relationship is almost always more important than the short-term problem.

Until you can retire on your savings, pensions and investments, your free social time will be limited. You must be able to divide this time wisely. Although many demands on your time will be urgent, you must also plan for the important. Little in your life will affect your overall well being more than building and maintaining strong personal relationships. Take a minute to write down the names of those in your social circle.

PRIORITIZE YOUR RESPONSIBILITIES

Your list might look like this:
1. Spouse   2. Children   3. Parents   4. Grandparents
5. Brothers/Sisters 6. In-laws   7. Cousins, Aunts and Uncles
8. Friends   9. Co-workers   10. Neighbors
11. Church members 12. Club members   13. Others

Now, you have a frame of reference for making decisions. For example, taking your family on a weekend get-away would be more important than a fishing trip with the guys from work. Taking your elderly mother shopping would be more important than helping your neighbor fix his car. These may not be the activities that you would prefer to do. These are the activities that you should be doing. The less needy you are the stronger your relationships may become. Start enjoying your trips to the bookstore and reading with the kids rather than always rushing

Ovid

to the golf course. Go to your neighbor's barbecue and ask if you can bring your sister who doesn't get many chances to go out on her own. You can still play golf. You can still have a drink after work with the gang. Just put your needs in their appropriate place. Be the best you. Two thousand years ago, the Roman poet Ovid had already figured out the secret to mastering relationships, *"To be loved, be lovable."*

HOW TO RESOLVE CONFLICT

To resolve a problem you must first confront the problem. Face the challenge. This simple act may require the most courage. To admit that you may be the offending party or at least partially responsible for the trouble is significant. How do you choose to handle criticism? Do you automatically fight or listen? Do you stop to consider the qualifications and motives of your critic? Are you able to stop and calmly restate your position? Attack the argument and not the person. Are you looking for solutions or to cast blame? Be serious and concise in stating your opinions. Don't rush. Get all the facts before you reach a decision. Don't argue in public.

You can learn an awful lot with your mouth closed and your ears open. Think about all the time and anguish you'll save by listening and immediately finding common ground on which to compromise. What does the other party consider a satisfactory resolution? If you ask and listen, the solution offered may be milder than you had imagined. Endeavor to keep lines of communication open.

There is a Danish proverb, which says, *"Wise men do not quarrel with each other."* Arguing often makes the other party become more defensive and want to dig-in and prevail. Take a time out. Figure out what is important to the other party. Is there a hidden agenda? Try to see the other person's side. Look for points of specific agreement and disagreement. Keep the discussion focused on the key issues. Are you both working from the same set of facts? May a third party be helpful in offering suggestions to resolve the conflict? Plant seeds based on your ideas. Remain calm and positive. Speak with respect. Don't be condescending. Look for compromise but when you're right, stand your ground. Decide. Smile. Move on. Someone has to be the bigger person and it can be you. You can't make peace without talking to your enemy. Say a prayer each day for all of the blessings that you have been given in life. Concentrate on what is right rather than who is right.

How far will you go to find harmony in your relationships? Can you flip a coin, share, give in, negotiate, take turns, agree, apologize, laugh, accept a mediator or pray?

SET YOUR PERSONAL BOUNDARIES

You don't have to put up with it. Who said that you should be a victim?

What is your threshold for inappropriate behavior? At home and at work, you have every right to establish limits to behaviors that you will not tolerate. These are your personal boundaries. Your children and subordinates should know these boundaries and you hope that your peers would not need to find them out. If anyone crosses the line, you should stop him or her immediately, explain your position and thank them for complying. If the behavior persists or reoccurs, you must demand that it stop. In a work situation, you should walk away and, if appropriate, report the incident. With children, there should be appropriate discipline. Your word must mean something.

Stick to your religious beliefs and to the Action Principles. You know the right thing to do. Do it. Do it for yourself and for those you love.

RELATIONSHIPS WITH FRIENDS

You can be happy with a few good friends. You can be happy with a few good acquaintances. Being a friend presumes a commitment while being an acquaintance does not. You do favors for friends. There is an Arabian proverb, which says, *"A friend is known when needed."* You consider doing favors for acquaintances. You want to listen to friends. You can excuse yourself with acquaintances. You must overlook weaknesses in friends. You can replace acquaintances.

You may hate going to funerals and hospitals and lending

money but you will do it all for a friend. Most people do not forget your acts of kindness toward them in their moments of need.

Some people need the strong emotional support of long friendships. They would feel lost without another kindred soul to discuss the highs and lows of life. They share their lives. Other quite happy people might find this close emotional bonding intrusive. They are quite content with acquaintance type relationships. They prefer a more private introspective lifestyle. They like to fish by themselves. They like to take a book to the park. They like to golf with the boys but don't want to be invited to the boys' grandson's birthday party. They are quieter people.

HOW TO REMEMBER NAMES

A good way to start making new friends is to get better at remembering names. People love the sound of their own name. Be known for your ability to remember names. With a little practice, it isn't that difficult. It will become a habit that can take you a long way. To remember a name, you must first hear the name. If you don't catch the name during the introduction, immediately ask to have the name repeated. Again, this isn't embarrassing to anyone, since people like the sound of their own name. As you shake hands, say the name, *"My pleasure to meet you Roberto. I'm Bill."* Try and say the name several times during your conversation. Before you leave this person, use this opportunity to give him one of your businesscards and to repeat his name again. *"Roberto, before you go, I'd like to give you one of my cards."* If he has a card, he will now give you one. *"Thank you, Roberto. Is your e-mail address on the card?"* This is the 21st century. When we want to establish networks, the easiest way is e-mail.

Since you will have a computer, you will want to use a contact manager program. This is an electronic version of an address book. Get in the habit of regularly recording the info from any new businesscards into your database. This will reinforce the name and face. If you are in a business where you may be exchanging a lot of cards, you may wish to invest in a small businesscard scanner. Just hearing and repeating names will take you a long way. Be prepared. Your friends will frequently ask to tap your extraordinary memory. And, you will have lots more friends.

RELATIONSHIPS WITH CHILDREN

Raising independent, mature, well-mannered children is one of life's great challenges. The Action Principles will provide the roots and wings. You must provide a strong moral and spiritual platform from which your children can grow. You must raise your children to become independent and self-reliant. You must work with them to develop a strong self-image based on a strong moral code. You do this with realistic praise and encouragement. You avoid false preaching and put-downs. Nothing will mean more than your good example.

The most important single thing that a father can do for his children is to love their mother.

Sometimes it may be tough to bring the entire family to weekly religious services. You go anyway. You can only pity the poor child who must face life's challenges without a belief in God channeled through a strong parental example.

Correcting your children's manners over and over again can get tedious. You do it anyway. Well-mannered children are welcomed anywhere and people do notice.

PARENTING ISN'T BARGAINING

Stop apologizing and making excuses for your children. Set limits and let them know the consequences for exceeding those limits. Meaning what you say is not being mean. If you aren't in charge, then every interaction between you and your child will dissolve into a deal making confrontation. They will only do one thing if you allow another. You will no longer be parenting but bargaining.

There is little doubt that giving your children everything cripples them. Just as you are tough, you can make your kids tough. If you have everything, you respect nothing. If nothing is ever hard to do, you can never become strong. Children should be given jobs and responsibilities with corresponding rewards and punishments as early as possible. A three-year-old can pick up his toys. A five-year-old can help carry the beach chairs to the car. A seven-year-old can make her bed and hang up her clothes. A ten-year-old can rake leaves and shovel snow. A sixteen-year-old can get a part time job. If a job is not done or not done satisfactorily, just as in the real world that they will inherit, there should be repercussions. You don't go to the mall. Your friend can't come for a sleepover. The repercussions should be simple and immediate. If you make and stick with your policies when the children are three years old, you will have many fewer problems when they are thirteen.

On occasion, you may have to discipline a child in public. This is almost unavoidable. Your long-term relationship with your well-behaved child is much more important than suffering the two-second sarcastic sneers of a few strangers who want to side with your child and make you feel like an abuser. Many more people will silently applaud and understand your firm verbal reaction to a child's inappropriate behavior. The world and your child will thank you later.

Teenagers may talk back to you once in awhile. Within reasonable limits, this is part of growing up and showing independence. Compromising between your fashion and entertainment sense and theirs is reasonable. Tardiness, foul language and a disregard for one's own possessions are not signs of adolescence or of any other age category. They are signs of the lazy and undisciplined. Well before the age of thirteen, clean clothes properly stored in a clean room and answering when called should be unspoken expectations.

No well-behaved child at any age should be allowed to talk back or shout at a parent or other elder. If a child asks to do something and you say no ten times and then yes the eleventh time, you will pay for the rest of your own life. Your word will mean little. Your future influence will be minimal. Your child will be in for a rude awakening and a very unpleasant life in the real world. You are condemning this child to a miserable life. He will be forever unsatisfied and probably unpopular.

BALANCE CHILDREN'S ACTIVITIES

Children don't have to be involved in three or four sports. Pick one. How about taking music or art or acting lessons? How about encouraging a child to volunteer? How about scouting? How about helping a child who wants to start a little business? A child can miss a soccer game if there is a greater benefit to the family as a whole. The child learns to sacrifice, to give and learns the high value placed on family. Family also means eating meals together with the television off and not grazing over snack foods and cereal.

Consider also coordinating children's activities so that during one quarter of the year all of the family is off on weekends and the family can take mini-vacations and trips on those free weekends. Get physical with walking, hiking, camping, boating and biking. Get cultural with museums, concerts, historical and travel tours. It can be done with planning.

Through your example, teach your children to respect their elders. Most adults are kind and would help your child in time of need. Most teachers and youth counselors are devoted to their careers, which means helping your children be all that they can be. If you want safe children, make them aware, and unafraid to confide in adults.

Average Is Not A Bad Word

Don't force your aspirations on your children. The apple doesn't fall far from the tree. If you and your spouse didn't get all A(s) in school why should your children? Encourage your children to do their best and let them know that their best is good enough.

If all the kids in the school are getting A(s) and B(s), this doesn't mean that the school is exemplary or that all the children in that school are miraculously superior to the norm. It only means that the grading policies are lax and that the children may be getting falsely inflated egos.

Every child who takes a test doesn't deserve a good grade. Every child who waddles onto a playing field doesn't deserve a trophy. Honesty and a dose of competition will serve them much better than false praise. Self-esteem is not an award. Without adult intervention, by age ten, children already know athletic, neat, funny and good looking from lazy, sloppy, boring and sarcastic. They know a real

"Don't disturb Daddy. He's busy visualizing unparalleled success in the business world and, by extension, a better life for us all."

award from a gift. They are already making their own choices.

Any child over the age of reason already knows not to walk in front of buses, swallow gasoline, bring weapons to school and jump from tall buildings. They also know not to take drugs, smoke cigarettes, abuse alcohol, speed in cars and engage in pre-marital sex. You don't have to tell them what they already know a thousand times. That would be easy if it worked. It doesn't work. What does work is your parental example, your values, your faith, your love and your involvement in their lives. Be there for them. Help them build the self-confidence to resist unwanted peer and societal pressures. Dare to be there for your children.

The average American child will have spent more time watching television before he goes to first grade than he will spend speaking with his father over the course of his entire lifetime. Fifty percent of children have television in their rooms and watch an average of twenty-eight hours of programs each week. Now add in more hours of telephone, video game and Internet time. You've got to start very young to help your children become selective in choosing positive activities over idle behavior. There is nothing wrong with a few hours of television or telephone or video games or Internet, but only after chores and homework and reading. Lead your children by example to make the right choices. The American author James Baldwin observed, *"Children have never been very good at listening to what their parents tell them but they never fail to imitate them."*

Where and from whom are your children learning about good music, art, literature, food and theater? Who is teaching them about the environment and conservation? How are they being introduced to the importance of kindness and generosity? To whom have you entrusted your children's character development? Teaching values by word and example is a parent's responsibility. Add your values to this short list.

A SHORT LIST OF UNIVERSAL VALUES

Courage	Loyalty	Trustworthiness	Respect
Kindness	Generosity	Discipline	Courtesy
Neatness	Thrift	Friendship	Determination
Persistence	Hard Work	Achievement	Punctuality
Pride	Responsibility	Reverence	

Children must also learn shame and regret when they are at fault especially concerning the feelings of others. As you treat your children, so will they become.

If you really want a superior child, instill in them a love of reading. Children read in families where they see the parents reading. Reading should be done in a place with minimal distraction without television or radio. Set a goal for your family reading time and then stick to it. Thirty minutes to forty minutes per day is reasonable. Make reading a family priority. When your family travels, everyone brings a book.

Give your children the opportunity to prove themselves. Don't deprive them of the joy of accomplishment. Make them work and they'll learn to appreciate more in their lives. Allow them to learn from their mistakes.

There is no time to wait. A lazy, ill-mannered child will not be able to compete globally. The advantages that some parents think that they are giving their children will fall woefully short if that child lacks character and self-discipline. Take the tough stands early. If your children learn the value of hard work and generosity, they will soar. Their lives will be happy. A twelve-year-old is old enough to understand and follow the Action Principles. A teen-ager can benefit from reading this book and the Master Success System.

Raising great kids will affect generations to come. Remain calm. Give your children the best gift you can – your time. When children are raised to be happy, content and self-reliant, they realize that doing good helps others and themselves.

If you raise your children according to a religious tradition, and you set a proper example, a wonderful thing will happen. You won't have to worry so much about them. They will be self-reliant, well mannered and both goal and service oriented. They will have learned from you to make the right choices. You will see success. They will be your children.

RELATIONSHIPS WITH BUSINESS ASSOCIATES

If you are a small business owner, you will want to hire as many people as possible who follow the Master Success System philosophy. You will gain a valuable employee. You also may have to be prepared for the day that that employee wishes to spread her own wings and start her own businesses. Wish her well.

Be careful what you say about yourself and your accomplishments because it is human nature for people to think the opposite. Bragging is counter-productive. When someone pays you a compliment, don't expand on it or excuse it, just say, *"Thank you."* You magnify a compliment's impact when you speak in terms of the recipient's action rather than your own opinions. If you are invited to a picnic and you like the fried chicken, rather than saying, *"Thank you, I love the chicken."* Instead say, *"I want to thank you. You did a wonderful job of preparing the chicken."*

Always be on the lookout for people who can advance your cause as partners, financiers, employees, consultants, mentors and investors. You can't possibly know everything or even enough to get everything done. You need others. Seek their counsel. Listen. Share the credit. Henry Ford could have thanked his mentor, Thomas Edison. George Lucas can thank his mentor, Francis Ford Coppola.

Communication is the key to good employee relations. Your policy must be honesty, openness and candor. This means for good or bad. Never tolerate laziness, disrespect, dishonesty or harassment. If an employee is not doing a proper job, the day he or she is terminated shouldn't come as a complete shock to them. As with children, don't make excuses to them or for them. Make a decision. Don't allow poor performance to linger or a poor work ethic to infect others. They had a job. They didn't do the job. This should not be your fault. It is their fault. If it is not their fault, then they are being blamed for something beyond their control and they are better off working somewhere that they are appreciated. People notice how you treat others.

Throughout the Master Success System, the concept of follow-up is repeated. It is important. Keep everyone informed and you go a long way toward minimizing any potential dissention or defection. The sales agent should call her homesellers every week to tell them of activity or reasons why there may be a lack of activity. The hairstylist can call a new client a week after the initial visit. The boss should check on a subordinate taking maternity leave. The teacher may trouble herself to call a parent two weeks after a conference with a progress report. These quick remembrances are habits of the successful. Follow-up

148

shows you care.

As you succeed and others notice, you may be called upon to speak. Whenever you have this opportunity to speak before any group, do not talk down to the audience. A condescending tone will immediately negate your efforts. Always treat everyone as important and they will hear your message.

HOW TO BUILD TEAMWORK

To build a strong team, whether that team concept is applied to a sport, family or business, individuals must subscribe to the principle of putting the team first. Each must be willing to make occasional personal sacrifices, respect one another and share the credit for the greater good of all. The team's mission must be outlined and understood through clearly defined goals. Individual strengths must be identified and appropriate roles assigned. Responsibility and accountability must be accepted. Ideas, suggestions, reasoned criticisms and questions must be encouraged. Those with experience must be willing to teach and assist beginners. Everyone commits to doing his or her individual and collective best to work to a high standard and, in a game, to better the competition and win. This requires a program of continuing education, practice and testing. When mistakes are made or games lost, the team must pull together to leave the past behind and move on to new challenges.

Booker T. Washington

If you are a team leader or coach, remember the words of Booker T. Washington, *"There are two ways of exerting one's strength: One is pushing down, the other is pulling up."*

YOUR RELATIONSHIP WITH GOD

You are one person among six billion on one planet of nine in a solar system of hundreds of thousands of solar systems. God is love and beauty and all that is good in man. When you see one person acting selflessly to benefit another, you see God. God is fun and happiness. He exists in every smile, laugh and twinkle in your eye. God is the one to thank every day for all the blessings that exist in your life.

If you actually do find hope and promise in the Master Success System and begin and keep with the program and ultimately find peace and prosperity in your life, it is God who gave you persistence and determination and the willingness to do all the hard work necessary to succeed. God has given you the free will to choose success. You must accept the calling to rise to your own potential. God has given you all that you need to Master Success. He made you the Master Piece. See that. Thank God.

OUR EXPERIMENT

Let's follow-up the experiment from earlier in the chapter. What would you do on your last day if you knew in advance that it was your last day? Would you go skydiving? Would you eat three great meals and enjoy every bite? Would you pray to God for forgiveness for your sins? Would you tell your wife and children that you loved them? Would you thank your employees and tell them how much you appreciate them? Would you arrange to donate your body to science or for organ transplants? Would you give money to someone who really needed it? Probably all of your answers are good valid answers. John Henry Cardinal Newman wrote, *"Fear not that thy life shall come*  *to an end, but rather fear that it shall never have a beginning."* Perhaps the best answer to this experiment, however, was the advice that the Roman Emperor Marcus Aurelius gave his people in the 2nd century, *"Live every day as if it were your last."* If you had the courage to live with this attitude, would you care about your material possessions or your personal relationships? Live fully today, expecting to die tomorrow.

Marcus Aurelius

KEY CONCEPTS

You can make the personal choice to be positive as you brush aside the minor daily annoyances that everyone faces. Be patient. Others notice those in control.

Listen for constructive criticism. You may learn of mistakes that you can correct. Life is teaching you a lesson if you pay attention. Guard against false praise. The master walks that middle line and is neither overly influenced by either criticism or praise.

To resolve conflicts ask yourself *"What does the other party consider a satisfactory resolution?"* If you ask and listen, the solution offered may be milder than you had imagined. Endeavor to keep lines of communication open. Remain calm and positive. Speak with respect. Don't be condescending. Look for compromise but when you're right, stand your ground.

At home and at work, you have every right to establish limits to behaviors that you will not tolerate. These are your personal boundaries. If anyone crosses the line, you should stop him or her immediately, explain your position and thank them for complying.

When raising children, take the tough stands early. If your children learn the value of hard work and generosity, they will soar. Their lives will be happy. A twelve-year-old is old enough to understand and follow the Action Principles. Give your children the best gift you can – your time.

Always be on the lookout for people who can advance your cause as partners, financiers, employees, consultants, mentors and investors. You can't possibly know everything or even enough to get everything done. You need others.

Communication is the key to good employee relations. Your policy must be honesty, openness and candor. This means for good or bad.

As you succeed and others notice, you may be called upon to speak. Always treat everyone as important and they will hear your message.

People love the sound of their own name. Be known for your ability to remember names. Get in the habit of regularly recording the info from any new businesscards into your database. This will reinforce the name and face.

Thank God for all he has done for you.

YOUR ASSIGNMENT

Your assignment for this chapter is for each day for the next twenty-one days to find a situation where you can exercise your self-control. It can be at home, at the office or on the road. Identify the moment. Restrain yourself. Breathe and relax. Let the moment pass. Feel stronger. Build your relationships.

CHAPTER TEN
MASTER LIFE

Every now and then go away and have a little relaxation.
To remain constantly at work will diminish your judgment.
Go some distance away, because work will be in perspective
and a lack of harmony is more readily seen.
Leonardo da Vinci, Florentine artist & scientist (b. 1452)

Your journey to success is a happy one. You are secure, confident and relaxed. You have made a conscious choice to enjoy your family, work, friends and your free time. You realize that success is not to be lived at some distant date. It is to be lived

now. You choose to be happy now. Life is too short to be unhappy. You are committed to living every day of your life with gusto. You understand Henry David Thoreau's words when he said, *"There is no value in life except what you choose to place upon it and no happiness in any place except what you bring to it yourself."* You have chosen to make your life a wonderful adventure. Living well is your reward.

Henry David Thoreau

You are a Renaissance person who finds beauty all the time and everywhere. You are reborn. The power to succeed is enlivening. You have this power. You realize that most of the best things in life are well within your budget. Your kind and generous nature will bring you an abundance of human warmth. People will like you. They will smile when they see you. You will have friends and family with whom you can share your success. You will eat right, exercise and put your head on the pillow each night with a clear conscience. Leave something for yourself. This is not being selfish. This is being successful. This is the advice of the English novelist D. H. Lawrence, *"Life is ours to be spent, not saved."*

Look to your Action Principles for guidance. Plan to have a good time. Laugh. Tell jokes. The *Koran* teaches, *"Blessed is he who makes his companions laugh."* Put variety and zest in your life. Set goals. Research. You think about what you really want and then you get it! A billionaire can't buy the good will that you possess and foster. A billionaire can't buy the happy life that you have decided to live. You appreciate all that you already have. Each day goes and will never return again. Don't wish away your life. Live it. You will feel much better doing things, being a person of action.

Fill your life with those things that make you happiest. Do you like baseball? Go to games. Do you like opera? Go to performances or listen to the Metropolitan Opera every Saturday afternoon on public radio. Do you love to grow cooking herbs? Go to your garden. Do you like rock climbing? Go to the mountains. Go to the movies. Take dancing lessons. Buy yourself a book or a new sweater. Take a bubble bath. Put on a CD. Have a glass of wine. You should have favorite authors, actors, singers, restaurants, designers, vacation spots, foods, walking trails, wines, television channels and sports. If not, start finding them. In the 3rd century, Saint Augustine preached, *"Decide to love and do what you like."* Seventeen hundred years later, the studies of Dr. Abraham Maslow led him to advise, *"A musician must make music, an artist must paint, a poet must write, if he is to be ultimately at peace with himself."*

Dr. Abraham Maslow

LIFE IS TO BE LIVED

The poet T. S. Eliot made a case for adventurous living when he said, *"Do not follow where the path may lead. Go instead where there is no path and leave a trail. Only those who will risk going too far can possibly find out how far one can go."* Successful living starts with your decision to do your best and not worry about the rest. Only when you are happy yourself will you be in the proper frame of mind to help others.

This is not a rehearsal. This is your one life. If you've been a saver and investor, the time comes when you should be freeing up some of that cash. Remember that the reason you made investments was not just to be rich but to lead a rich lifestyle. Take some of your profits and enjoy them. Unless you have a handicapped child to provide for, leav-

T. S. Eliot

ing a large estate for others to spend when you're gone doesn't make much sense. There is nothing sadder than a rich miser who only lives to count his money. The 18th century English poet Dr. Samuel Johnson said, *"It is better to live rich than to die rich."*

Dr. Samuel Johnson

Work hard, sacrifice, save, invest and it all leads to enjoyment. Perhaps you've started thinking about the choices you've been making in your life with an eye toward simplicity. Can you get by with one less car or a used car? Can you move to a less expensive neighborhood? Is last year's coat or last year's hat still wearable? Are you willing to work a little extra overtime? Will you bag your lunch on four days to splurge on the fifth day? You don't necessarily have to make a high income to enjoy a high quality life. Rich is a state of mind.

Free time for enjoyment. Look forward to being happy. Anticipation can be a wonderful feeling. Program enjoyment time into all of your schedules. Take a couple of nights off and a full day off each week. Take a full weekend off each month and go on a mini-vacation. Take a week off every three or four months and take a real vacation. Again, it won't happen unless you plan for it to happen and then you must jealously guard your plan. Consider the words of Leonardo da Vinci that opened this chapter.

SPOIL YOURSELF

Make a point of spoiling yourself on a regular basis. The American novelist Christopher Morley said, *"There is only one success – to be able to live your life in your own way."* There should be some activities and gifts just for you. Next, there should be activities that you share just with your spouse. Then, there should be family activities. Then, the next circle goes to friends and church groups and clubs, etc. Plan for it all.

As you reach your financial goals, can you cut back your time at work? Can you work a four-day week or work part-time? If you enjoy your work, maybe you'll want to stay with working part-time and playing part-time. Maybe you want to work your hardest until you can retire and then train for the senior pro golf tour. Perhaps, you want to retire or work part-time and spend the rest of your time writing music. You decide. Go fishing.

Paint a watercolor. Make a quilt. Have a beer with the boys. Sing in the chorus. Watch pro wrestling. Live your life doing a lot of things that you enjoy doing and you will find that work and being nice to others is much easier. You are happy.

Think of the Action Principles as your magic wand.

You can buy a sports car. You can dine in the best restaurants. You can tour Europe. You can hear the world's greatest singers. You can stay in the best hotels. You can buy an antique dining room set. When it comes to your happiness, everything doesn't have to be discount and cut rate.

If you really want a brand new luxury sports car, you save and buy it. If this is something that you really want, this isn't an unreasonable or frivolous goal. It is what you want and what you want is important. You can't afford everything all the time but you can probably afford this single luxury. Even if the car costs a year's pay, it is your money and it is what you've decided to get as a result of your hard work. You can join car clubs associated with the vehicle and go to rallies. You can read books and articles. You can find websites and newsgroups. Probably, in your research, you'll come across a used car at a great price. Maybe you'll decide to restore a car. It doesn't even have to be a great investment. Everything doesn't have to be a great investment. It can just be what you want.

The foolish move would be to buy an expensive car or clothes or jewelry or anything for status. The law of opposites strikes again. Snobbery creates the reverse effect one intends. Buy for yourself and not for others. Most people are focused on themselves and not on your scarf or your shoes. You work too hard to waste your money. Be sure that you really want what you think you want.

GET UP AND GO

How about taking a trip to Europe? You don't have to wait until you're in your sixties or seventies. You can go now. If you are willing to travel during the off season, you may pay a half or even a third of the full peak summer price. Don't worry. Westminster Abbey, the Vatican and Amsterdam canals are there all year round. The people will be smiling in Dublin. The food will be great in Paris. With planning, many can afford this type of trip. Consider house swaps and staying in bed and breakfasts or youth hostels. Many churches and local civic groups organize affordable tours. Go to MasterSuccess.com for links to bargain travel websites. Can you travel to Mexico or the Caribbean during the summer and save a bundle? Of course. Most hotels offer weekend travel packages that may include food, transportation and entertainment. Get going.

Why don't most people do this? Because it isn't in their mind-set. Because they haven't researched. Because they haven't planned. This is them. This is not you.

THE INTERNET

This is the 21st century. You can't be a success without a computer. If you have to work to get one, do that. It won't take you long. You need your own computer and not the library's or a friend's or the kid's. Find and buy the fastest Internet hook-up you can afford. If your cable or phone company offers high speed Internet access, sign up. This book is only an introduction to all the benefits you will receive as a member of the Master Success System. Find out about it all on our website at MasterSuccess.com. Be there. This is for you.

The Internet is not only a wonderful business and research tool but it is also a great tool for life enrichment. All major newspapers are now on-line and offer extensive entertainment and cultural listings. Anything you ever wanted to know about any movie, play, CD, museum, sport, hobby or concert is all only a click away from any search engine.

PERSONAL PAMPERING

You can get into excellent physical condition just doing sit-ups and push-ups in your room at home, but you should investigate the health clubs in your area. See people in great shape and be inspired to improve. Maybe you'll make some friends and maybe you'll do some networking. There will be many cross-training opportunities to help you stay motivated. You'll be able to work out by yourself or take classes from step-aerobics to bicycle spinning to cardio-kickboxing. There will be staff, to ask questions on fitness and nutrition. There will be personal trainers. If you are just beginning an exercise program, personal trainers can be a good idea. They will be there to help you plan a practical exercise routine. They will show you how to exercise correctly. And, most importantly, they will be there waiting for you so you will have to be there. After your workout, relax in the whirlpool or steam or sauna. If you like, get a massage. Joining a health club will prove very cost effective for you since you will use it so often. As you sit in the hot tub give a moment of thanks to all those members who join and then don't come. They are the ones subsidizing your regular visits. Remember the list of life sports. Choose one and stick with it.

Go outside and smell the roses. Get out into the fresh air. Walk, hike, camp, swim, bike, climb and garden. Some of the best things in life are free or inexpensive. Take a book to the park. Feed the pigeons. Look at the trees, flowers and stars. If you haven't seen the magnificence of a sunrise or sunset recently, do that. Would your children or grandchildren like to join you? How about bringing the dog? Take a deep breath, exhale slowly and feel the exhilaration of being successful. Your journey is a beautiful one.

Take good care of your body. If your personal hygiene is suspect, no one is going to be thinking about how successful you are. Dress well. Smile. Stand up straight and put confidence in your posture. You are now beautiful. You are now handsome. The confidence you feel inside will shine on the outside.

You can afford to pamper yourself. If you want to have your hair cut, dyed, straightened or curled every few weeks, do that. Do whatever makes you feel good. What type of clothing do you look best wearing? What types of glasses flatter your face? What colors suit your skin tone? Ask the experts. Ask your friends. Look in magazines and on the Internet. Be proud to look your best. If you have to work an extra hour or two to pamper yourself, do that. Go have a manicure or an herbal facial or wear a freshly laundry starched shirt every day. Do anything that makes you feel special. You are special. You work hard. You are worth it.

Be sure that you use what you buy. Maybe you can't have or don't want a closet full of expensive suits and shoes but you can afford one or two of the best. Buy the best. Choose a few personal luxuries and enjoy them. Take good care of shoes and apparel and they will serve you well for a long time. If you choose, you can afford one or two pure silk ties or scarves. If you choose, you can afford a high quality perfume or cologne. If you are going to buy one winter coat that you will wear almost every day, invest in a nice one. Do you need three or four winter coats? No, you don't. But, if you love fashion and it really makes you happy and you are willing to sacrifice other things for it, then, go for it. Life enrichment is what you say it is. You are an original. Act like one. If you like wild ties or red sports cars or fancy fingernails or singing in the shower, go for it. A little eccentricity is interesting and appealing. The operative word is *"little."*

Enjoy your days. Don't watch television while you're eating dinner. Instead, light a candle. Open a bottle of wine. Put on a CD. Speak of pleasant things that happened during the day and

Johann Wolfgang Von Goethe

events and plan family outings and vacations. Your family and friends are a blessing. Be with them whenever and as often as you can. Two hundred years ago, the German poet Johann Wolfgang Von Goethe wrote, *"One ought, every day at least, to hear a little song, read a good poem, see a fine picture, and, if it were possible, to speak a few reasonable words in order that worldly cares may not obliterate the sense of the beautiful which God has implanted in the human soul."*

COMMUNITY RESOURCES

Be sure to patronize the cultural activities in your own community. Every ticket to every worthwhile event doesn't have to cost a day's pay. Are there plays and concerts and film festivals sponsored by the schools, colleges, churches, libraries and private groups in your community? Are there lots of local sporting events? Of course. Join in. Pack a picnic lunch. Bring the family. Thank the people in charge and the performers. Support culture and sports with your ticket purchases and your letters to the editor. Be a part of your community. What can you do to make where you live a better place? What can you organize? How about making a difference by running for office?

A fail proof way to enrich your life is by helping others. You can't go wrong doing right. Here is a small example. Pick a nursing home on your way home. Stop for twenty minutes with a bucket of candy for the residents and staff. Yes, the candy may cost you $20 or $30 a week. You can afford this. Yes, many will wonder how and why you do this. You say little. Others talk. You act. Do you do it for the many friends you'll make? Do you do it for all the *"thank yous"* you'll receive? You really do it because it will make you feel so good. You do it because it needs to be done and no one else is doing it. You can do this. You do this because of the Golden Rule. You do this because you wouldn't want to be eighty or ninety years old and forgotten by everyone except a few who are paid minimum wage to be with you. You do the hard things. Jesus of Nazareth taught us all with his words and by his example, *"Do unto others as you would have them do unto you."* Now, you set the example.

ADULT EDUCATION

It would be difficult to envision a fully enriched life lived in isolation. Being mindful is the opposite of being mindless. To fully appreciate life you must be conscious of current events. Think about how national and international events may impact your personal life or business for better or worse. You should be in the habit of reading a daily newspaper and watching the nightly news. You should be aware of the offerings on public television and commercially produced documentaries and news specials. You should find one or more like-minded people with whom you can intelligently discuss the issues of the day. If you belong to a health club, you can do your aerobic work and watch the news, read a paper, or listen to a motivational or business tape.

Most communities and colleges sponsor adult education programs suited to a wide range of interests. These courses are usually offered during convenient evening hours for you to learn from and enjoy. Local experts seeking to share a joy in a subject often teach these courses.

READING IS EVERYTHING

President Thomas Jefferson admitted, *"I cannot live without books."* Supreme Court Justice Oliver Wendell Holmes wrote, *"Man's mind, once stretched by a new idea, never regains its original dimensions."* You can't be a smart person without reading. Read for current events. Read for business. Read for enjoyment. For one person that means reading more non-fiction and for others it means best sellers, classics, mysteries, science

Oliver Wendell Holmes

fiction or romance. Just read. Let your children see you reading. Challenge yourself. Rene Descartes , the 17th Century French philosopher, wrote *"The reading of all good books is like a conversation with all the finest men of past centuries."* If you read one book a month on a specific subject, in four years you will be a world authority on that subject – not well read, not well informed but an authority. A-B-A-B – Always Bring A Book. If

you get stuck in a line, take out your book. If you have to wait for any appointment, take out your book. Rather than getting upset, learn something. Mark Twain made an important point when he said, *"A man who does not read books has no advantage over the man who can't read them."* And the American humorist Will Rogers observed, *"A man only learns in two ways, one by reading, and the other by association with smarter people."*

Will Rogers

The world is such a wonderful place. If you want to learn how to cook, sail, garden, golf, draw, act, sing or write, there are plenty of people who are ready, willing and able to teach you. Almost everywhere there are in-person adult education opportunities at schools and colleges. Almost everything that you ever wanted to learn about anything can be found on the Internet or in books and magazines. Almost any hobby or sport

that you can conceive will have an association, club or group already in place.

When you are relaxing and enjoying your life, when you are content that you have done your best, you are mastering success.

CREATE YOUR PERSONAL SPACE

"This is so great - I'm home." Make your home your personal oasis. Surround yourself with whatever makes you happy. Get comfortable. If you love candles and incense, burn

away. Fill your space with flowers, art prints, photographs and good music. One person will love log cabins and another oriental rugs. Live in the city or the suburbs or the country. It doesn't matter. One person's hand-me-down junk is another man's antiques. The important thing is that you think about making your environment comfortable for you. You don't just end up with things; you choose the furniture and accessories and wall coverings that you like. Maybe, in one house, all you can call your own is a small room, even a corner of basement. In another situation, the whole house or apartment or condo may be yours to decorate. At estate sales and auctions, you may be able to find excellent quality furnishings at reasonable prices.

Is there anything that you can do with your car or office? If you have confidence making these decisions, make them. If not, hire an interior decorator or ask a friend whose style you admire for help.

THROW PARTIES

You enjoy your own company during your quiet times. You should also enjoy sharing time with family and friends. Today, too many people lead lives that are too disorganized or they are too cheap or they have been abused too often in the past to throw a party, even a dinner party. If you are truly with friends, you should be able to lay back a little and enjoy your own party. Organize picnics. Have a backyard barbecue. The menu doesn't have to be perfect. The wine selection doesn't have to be just right. If the idea of a party creates anxiety, you are throwing the wrong kind of party or inviting the wrong people. Also, as a host or hostess, you have every right to stipulate when the party begins and when the party ends. If you cannot say, *"It's 10:00 and the party's over,"* don't have parties.

BE SPONTANEOUS

You do have to plan for your happiness to happen. However, a little spontaneity will add zing to your life. Loosen up. Every once in a while bring home flowers for no good reason. Take everyone to dinner without making elaborate plans. Give the office an afternoon off and bring everyone to the movies. Call a meeting at the beach. Rent a convertible for the weekend. Promote dress down Fridays. Take the kids for miniature golf and an ice cream. Grab a mental health day just for yourself.

KEY CONCEPTS

This is it. This is your one life. Plan to have a good time. Your life will be full of variety and zest. Set goals. Research. Think about what you really want and then get it! Fill your life with those things that make you happiest.

Successful living starts with your decision to do your best and not worry about the rest. The best road to helping others is to be happy yourself. Free time for enjoyment. It won't happen unless you plan for it to happen so make enjoyment part of your plan.

If you really want something, save your money and buy it. What you want is important. If you are careful in your spending most of the time you can afford to buy those expensive things that you want most. Make your home your personal oasis. Surround yourself with whatever makes you happy. Everything doesn't have to be a great investment. Just make sure that those things you buy are what you really want most and not some status symbols you've been talked into getting.

Many great things may not even be that expensive. If you want to travel you can find ways to travel at a reasonable price. There are plays and concerts and film festivals for little or no cost available in many areas.

Reading is the key. If you read one book a month on a specific subject, in four years you will be an authority on that subject. A-B-A-B – Always Bring A Book. If you have to wait for any appointment, take out your book. Rather than getting upset, learn something.

Don't lose your spontaneity. You don't have to plan everything. If you want to do something go for it. Success means enjoying what you have earned.

YOUR ASSIGNMENT

Your assignment for this chapter is to read this book and at least one other book during the next 21 days. During this time, start the habit of always bringing a book (A-B-A-B) with you. When you have free time, start learning or enjoying with your book. Also, for each day of the next three weeks, re-read five of the Action Principles.

CHAPTER ELEVEN
MASTER ALLIANCES

The more I help others to succeed, the more I succeed.
Ray Kroc, Founder, McDonald's Corporation (b. 1902)

Throughout this book, you have read about the power of self-reliance and how to develop the skills related to personal mastery. This is true. At the same time, you have seen the value in seeking the support of others as you work toward bringing peace and prosperity into your own life. Now, it may be important for you to seek even more help. Quietly behind the scenes, many successful people have partners, allies or mentors playing a central role in their personal goal planning, day to day work activities and accomplishments. Hopefully, in Chapter One, you identified such a person, called him or her and are now anxious to meet and to start discussing your ideas and action plans.

In researching why other personal development and self help courses often fail to bring about the anticipated results, you will see that the primary reason most people do not succeed is that they fail to follow the recommendations. It's not that the ideas were flawed; it's that there was no check and balance system to assure their execution. According to Napoleon Hill, considered by many the most important self-help writer of the 20th century, only one reader in a hundred ever followed through on his advice and become successful. Most motivational writers will honestly admit how difficult it is to get people to take action even when that action is clearly in their own best interest. Reading is easy. Making life changes and working hard is something else.

As you have learned, you can't change someone unless that person wants to be changed and is willing to put forth the effort to change. If you are in that one percent of self-motivated individuals who can go it alone, fine. If you feel that you may be someone who could benefit from a little nudge now and then, you may want to consider putting yourself on the line by sharing your hopes, dreams and disappointments with another person. Psychological research has shown that when a person tells someone else about their plans, they are far more likely to stick to those plans. In other words, you find someone you trust and then you give that person permission to encourage, motivate or prod you into doing what you said you intend to do. If you are lucky, this person may be an excellent source for insights, referrals and recommendations. At the very least, this person can serve as a sounding board for your ideas and intentions.

There are three ways people can help you master success:

1. Partner. The ideal situation is a partner who is supportive of you and is practicing the Master Success System himself or herself.

2. Ally. The next best is an ally who is supportive of you even if he or she does not wish to commit personally to the system.

3. Mentor. A person who has done or is doing what it is that you want to do and is willing to guide you.

To begin, anyone agreeing to help you should be encouraged to read this book. You might want to invest in several copies. The first copy of this book is always $19.95 and all additional copies ordered at the same time are always only $10.00 each. Remember that the American Success Institute is a non-profit organization and all the books you purchase, all the courses you take, all the people you tell about our work will not only help you but will help us to help others. The best way to order books is on-line at MasterSuccess.com. Having read the book, they will realize your intentions and also be better prepared to offer suggestions based on the Master Success book and the Action Principles.

WHAT TO LOOK FOR IN A PARTNER

A partner is someone who is also on the journey to Master Success. You will both work on your assignments and goal setting exercises. You will meet regularly and exchange information and positive suggestions in a supportive environment. You are there to offer positive reinforcement and encouragement to each other. You both stand to achieve more with the help of each other. A fellow student or co-worker, friend or spouse may be a willing partner.

Select a partner whose style and attitude is compatible with your own. If you subscribe to the philosophy of the Action Principles, you will expect that your partner will also. You should expect that your partner would seek the same work/family/social balance as you do. You should expect that your partner would have the same core values as you. If you both are in the same industry this can be useful but not necessary. A business partner is different from a success partner. If you own a business and have business partners, hopefully you would organize your business around the Master Success philosophy and the Action Principles. Your business partners may or may not make good success partners. It is more likely that since you are looking for fresh objectivity and a neutral atmosphere that a success partner will not be closely tied to you as an investment partner in a particular business.

Be wary of choosing a gloom and doom type partner with a negative attitude. Your partner should be someone who believes that change is possible, that people can grow through learning. Conversely, a perpetually perky yes-person would likewise be of little significant long-term benefit. You want someone who is open to possibilities while at the same time being tough minded and realistic. In other words, they will provide support for any credible plan but they'll be willing to provide a reality check if someone makes you a *"too good to be true"* offer. You want someone who will help you solve problems, whom you can bounce your ideas off and who will provide frank and honest commentary. Choose a Partner who is willing to push you toward your potential. Feel free to form your own mutual admiration society where you nurture and encourage each other's efforts. Success partnerships can involve more than two people. You may form a small group.

WHAT TO LOOK FOR IN AN ALLY

Just as with a Partner, an ally must be supportive and positive.

An ally is someone you know and trust. It can be an old friend, your brother or sister, your mother or father. An ally can be your favorite clergy person or teacher. Often a spouse is a good choice. It is someone that you would feel comfortable confiding in without fear of ridicule or argument. The motivation of your ally is to be your number one fan and cheer you on to success. Thank them often. If you see little gifts they'd like, buy them. Anyone who will take the time to listen to your dreams and plans and keep you pointed in the right direction is a valuable asset. Treasure them.

The difference between a partner and an ally is that the ally is not particularly interested in participating fully in the Master Success System. Also, an ally is usually more interested in you personally than in your business acumen and earning potential. The ally may feel more comfortable than a partner or mentor in telling you that you look too tired or you're getting too fat or that you should spend more time at home. An ally can be a source for tough advice that you may not hear elsewhere. You may find that an ally, having seen your progress, will eventually become interested in learning more about the Master Success System. At that point they may make the transition from ally to partner.

You can work with both partners and allies. You decide what support you need and what potential candidates are available.

What to Look for in a Mentor

The best place to find a mentor is through the trade association associated with your industry. Look for those associations on-line or in library directories. Attend meetings and start networking. Pay particular attention to retired association members who may have years of experience and a database full of contacts. Retired members may have the time and inclination to meet you for breakfast and lunch brainstorming sessions. They may even be willing to work for you part-time or in a consulting capacity.

There are government mentoring programs available, such as S.C.O.R.E., to help fledgling business owners. S.C.O.R.E. has helped many budding entrepreneurs. They may have a good match for you. However, they may not. If you want to become a dress designer then you may not get all the help you need from a well meaning former oil company executive. In this situation, you might be able to glean some general business advice but very little advice specific to your business. If you are following the Master Success System, you should be capable of doing your own research and finding your own mentor. You ask and keep asking. There are wonderful retired people out there just waiting to be asked. They aren't hard to find. Again, can you imagine the contacts and advice of someone who has been in your business for 30-40-50 years? Most retired people will be happy to continue to make a positive contribution to someone with your positive attitude.

If there is any shortcut to mastering success, this may be it. If you keep your eyes and ears open to opportunity, you will find knowledgeable, experienced people willing to help you along your journey.

AS A PARTNER YOU COMMIT TO:

Read Master Success.
Do all the exercises in the book.
Exchange with your partner copies of your goals.
Exchange with your partner copies of your personal and business mission statements.
Exchange with your partner copies of your weekly plan.
Meet weekly.
Call or e-mail each other once during the week to compare notes and check on progress.

AS AN ALLY YOU COMMIT TO:

Read Master Success.
Meet weekly or bi-weekly.
Review the previous week's plan.
Preview a copy of your friend's weekly plan.
Offer constructive advice and criticism.

AS A MENTOR YOU COMMIT TO:

Read Master Success.
Meet with your advisee at least once per month.
Discuss specific business problems.
Offer constructive advice and criticism.

BEFORE EACH MEETING

Throughout the week you should carry pen and paper and jot down thoughts and ideas that relate to your next meeting with your partner, ally or mentor. If you are working with a partner, this means that you will be looking for ideas from both your perspective and theirs. Get in the habit of clipping business articles to read and distribute. If it is in a book, highlight points of interest. If it is a really important book, buy several copies to distribute.

The purpose of the meeting is not social but to work on your success plan. As with your quiet time, try to choose a regular time and place for your meeting where the chances for being interrupted will be minimized. The format for meetings with allies and mentors may be a little more flexible and informal. Plan on your meetings running from thirty to sixty minutes. Stick to your agenda and spend about ten minutes on the primary objective topic. Keep the conversation moving.

Each partner's meeting should include:

1. Progress report – What have you done in the past week to move towards your major goals? Report on promises and commitments made at previous meeting.

2. Review plan - Review items from weekly plan that were not done during the previous week.

3. Discussion - Discuss ways your Partner can overcome his or her specific difficulties and accomplish the previous week's goals. Partner recommits to undone items and puts them on his new weekly plan.

4. Brainstorming - You and your partner discuss new ideas and work on coming up with solutions to problems. The idea is to think big, to throw out any idea that comes to mind. This is a powerful tool for devising innovative and creative insights and new plans.

5. New To-do list - Tell Partner about a minimum of 3 new to-do items and commit to do them. Give your partner a copy of your list. To-do items should be clear. Your partner should be able to easily determine whether you have done them or not at the next meeting. *'Think about real estate'* is not a clear to-do item. *'Look at five properties'* is more definite and accountable.

6. Schedule the next meeting – The real value in your meetings will take place over the course of time. Be patient. Be sure to plan your next meeting date and arrange for any follow-up calls and e-mails.

7. Be sure to say, *"Thank you."* - Let there be no question that your partners, allies or mentors understand that you appreciate their interest and input.

Agenda for Your First Meeting:

The agenda for your first meeting will vary from subsequent meetings. During your first meeting, you will describe your enthusiasm for the Master Success System and explain the personal changes and actions that you are about to undertake. To better understand your objectives, you will give your partner, ally or mentor a copy of Master Success. If you are working with someone who is a partner, you will ask them to commit to a meeting once a week. You will give your partner a copy of your weekly plan and you will discuss what you intend to accomplish for that week. You will set-up a specific time and date for your next meeting.

At each subsequent meeting, you will follow the regular agenda and discuss a specific topic based on the appropriate chapter from the book. After the tenth meeting, you can repeat the meeting objective agendas. The following are only suggestions:

Meeting 2 Goal setting   Meeting 3 Planning
Meeting 4 Financial analysis   Meeting 5 Time analysis
Meeting 6 Income analysis   Meeting 7 Investments
Meeting 8 Real estate   Meeting 9 Health
Meeting 10 Quarterly review

Master Success Groups

In your journey towards success you will have many questions. You will discover that you need the assistance of people with specialized knowledge about a wide variety of subjects: business, computers, the Internet, stocks, real estate, health and many others. Go to your local library and surf the Internet. Adult education courses and local civic groups are good resources. Our two websites, MasterSuccess.com and Dojo.com contain a great deal of practical information together with links to much more. You can find people who are already successful at doing whatever you now want to do. You can call local trade associations. You can attend conferences, lectures and conventions. Find a way.

As a member of the Master Success system you have another resource available to help you in your journey: Master Success Groups. It is our intention to help groups of interested individuals form groups with the common goal of achieving peace and prosperity through the Master Success System.

As the concept of Master Success Groups develops, you will find opportunities to:

NETWORK:

The Master Success Groups will bring action-oriented people together. If you need an electrician perhaps there is one in your group. Or someone may have a good recommendation. Do you need a reliable auto mechanic? Perhaps a member knows one. Do you want to invest in the stock market? There's a good chance that if you ask around at a Master Success Group meeting you will find several people already doing what you want to do.

MOTIVATION:

Groups are a source of motivation. Meeting with like-minded people every month and learning of their successes is invigorating. You are not alone. Share your stories and tips.

ANSWERS:

At the group meetings you will hear the solutions others have found to common problems. What software do others use? Where do they buy their computers? How do they do their taxes?

When a group of people with common purpose gather together they form an alliance that is greater than the sum of its parts. Just as your partner motivates you to succeed so too will your allies in the group.

Once you and your Partner have finished reading Master Success you will want to find out if there is a Master Success group in your area.

POSSIBLE SPECIAL INTEREST GROUPS:

Charitable/Volunteer Groups	Investment Groups
Computer User Groups	Real Estate Groups
Entrepreneur Groups	Marketing Groups
Youth Groups	Sports/Health Groups
Community Improvement Groups	Reading Groups

A TYPICAL MEETING'S FORMAT

Master Success Groups will be encouraged to hold general meetings once a month. They may run other specialized meetings as well. Meetings may be held in public libraries, schools, colleges or public buildings like city hall. Smaller groups may meet at restaurants.

Meetings are free. They are local.

Meetings should be 60 - 90 minutes long.

30 minutes: Networking, announcements, and refreshments

10 minutes: Introduction of new members, brief member comments

20 minutes: Guest speaker

10 minutes: Q&A and discussion with speaker

20 minutes: Miscellaneous

In addition to meetings, groups may also arrange for discounts with local businesses. They can provide volunteer telephone help on various subjects. Some groups may wish to run e-mail lists where people can be in constant touch brainstorming and discussing their plans. They can provide local support for people creating specialized new groups. To find if anyone has started a Master Success Group in your area, go to MasterSuccess.com. If you are interested in starting a group, go to the website and obtain the Group Director's Resource Kit that offers practical advice and tips on recruiting members, finding speakers, fundraising, organizing meetings, etc.

KEY CONCEPTS

Many successful people can attribute much of their success to the encouragement and guidance of others. You can do the same by working with a partner, ally or mentor. A partner is someone who is also taking the Master Success journey to peace and prosperity. An ally is a close personal acquaintance and your #1 booster. A mentor is a seasoned pro who is doing or has done what it is that you want to do. Your objective is to meet with these helpful advisors on a regular basis to discuss your plans, your progress and to brainstorm new possibilities.

As the Master Success System develops, Master Success Groups will form where motivated individuals who are following the Action Principles can meet to network, learn from local experts and exchange ideas.

YOUR ASSIGNMENT

Follow up on your assignment for Chapter One. Set up a meeting with your partner, ally or mentor and proceed as described above.

CHAPTER TWELVE
MASTER SUCCESS 2

*Be of a good cheer. Do not think of today's failures, but of
the success that may come tomorrow. You have set your-
selves a difficult task, but you will succeed if you persevere; and you will find a joy in overcoming obstacles.
Remember, no effort that we make to attain something
beautiful is ever lost.*
Helen Keller, American essayist and lecturer (b.1880)

You have now started on your journey. The horizon is bright.
If you have read Master Success, have read the Action Principles,
and are working on the assignments, you have a good idea of
what it takes to succeed.

You have set goals, made plans and created a mission statement. You have examined ways to spend your time more productively. You have critically evaluated your job and earning
potential. You have reviewed your budget and savings program.
You have considered the possibilities of real estate investing.
You have thought about your health in terms of diet, exercise
and self-defense. You have reflected on the value of meditation
and negotiation and prayer and forgiveness. You have re-exam-
ined the importance of your family and other personal relationships. You have investigated educational, cultural and recreational opportunities in your community. You are weighing the
advantages of working with a partner, ally or mentor.

This is how you'll know if the message of Master Success has
reached you.

When you want to roll over on that cold morning but instead
get up and go to the gym, in that defining moment, you are
mastering success. When you decide to buy a less expensive car
and invest the difference, in that defining moment, you are mastering success. When you decide to go to your daughter's dance
recital rather than to the ball game with your friends, in that
defining moment, you are mastering success. When you take the

family to church, when you donate to charity, when you volunteer at the food pantry, when you begin to correct a bad habit, when you thank a veteran, when you stand up for a person being treated unfairly, when you sit down with a lonely person, in all of these defining moments, you are mastering success. Through these defining moments that you face every day, through your own free will and choice, ignoring the fact that there may be an easier option, you live as a master of success. This is the journey.

On this journey, you don't have to change who you are. You can love expensive champagne or a six pack of beer or both or neither. You can love going out and being the life of the party or prefer quieter evenings at home. Personality types, lifestyle choices and material possessions do not differentiate those on the journey from those wandering aimlessly through life. People on the journey have simply made the choice to be happy and content right now with each step. Happiness and contentment, peace and prosperity result from your conscious choice to improve yourself and to help others. Everything else is in God's hands.

The words in this book could not have changed you. That would be too easy. If anything, these words simply sparked or rekindled a flame that always existed. Will you let that flame burn ever brighter or will you allow it to sputter out?

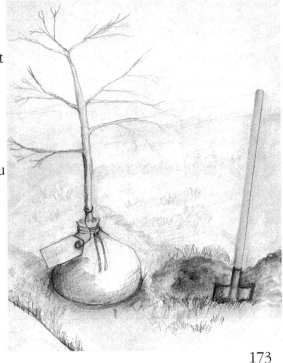

Maybe up until now you haven't been the best student or athlete or the hardest worker or the kindest person. No one expects more from you than you expect from yourself. Is there some greatness within you that you have allowed to lie dormant and have kept so well camouflaged for so many years? Are you now ready to bring this powerful new you forward? You're going to surprise a lot of people. Yes, that would be wonderful.

Do you even know your

own potential? Run for governor, try out for the senior golf tour, make your neighborhood drug free, write a hit song, clean up a river, console a friend, retire early or earn a fortune. What can't you do?

If you decide to master success, there are only two things that can stop you immediately and permanently in your tracks: laziness and selfishness. Barring these two fatal flaws, the world and everything wonderful about it awaits you. The rewards of mastering success are worth all the risks and all the sacrifices and all the hard work. You are an individual. You don't have to wait for the approval of others. Now is your time. You don't have to wait for opportunity. This is the opportunity. Be who you want to be. Do what you want to do. It is your one life to live and no one else's. You are a strong individual. If you have money and degrees and contacts, use them. If you haven't got them, get them or go around them. Find a way. Make a plan. Easy or hard doesn't matter; you will still do it. Be honest. No envy. No excuses.

You are a strong, determined individual. You may face prejudice and ridicule and physical pain and emotional distress. Disasters may knock you down. You may make big mistakes. But you quietly survive. You think and you reason and you take action. You take quiet comfort in your continual commitment to do your best for yourself and for those you love. You are in control. You are a strong, determined, kind individual. You choose to take a principle-centered approach to solving personal and professional problems. You listen and forgive. You focus on what others want and somehow end up with everything that you've ever needed.

When you commit your life to continual self-improvement and helping others, it doesn't matter where you start and there is no telling where you will end up. It doesn't matter if you are sitting in a stretch limo or in a wheelchair. It doesn't matter if you live in an affluent suburb or a country trailer park. It doesn't matter if you have the physique of an athlete or have just lost two hundred pounds and still need to lose another three hundred. No one can tell how tough or successful you are simply by seeing the outside you. It is what is inside of you and what you do with your God given talents that will make the difference. Don't give up. Let the Action Principles lead you to write your goals, make your plans, list your to-dos and make today and every day special. Push yourself. Make yourself do the hard things. Live a full, rich, rewarding life. Inspire others by your quiet example. At the end of the day, you can relax tired but satisfied and happy that you have done your best. This is mastering success.

Be the best that you can be because you can't conceive of living any other way. Stand tall. You will be surrounded by genuine affection from your husband, wife, children, friends and co-workers. Even strangers will react positively to you, having sensed your confidence. Love, friendship, respect, peace and prosperity will be yours to live and enjoy every day. In trying, you are a master of success. This may all seem miraculous to you but it will just be your following God's plan and, in this defining moment, committing to improving yourself and helping others.

You are really going to like this journey. I'll see you at MasterSuccess.com,

Bill

The Action Principles

~1~

Set Goals

Unless you shape your life, circumstances will shape it for you. You have to work, sacrifice, invest, and persist to get the results you want. Choose them well. You can't start your planning until you know where you want to go.

You are the sculptor of your own image. Have others already done what you want to do? Study them and do what they did. Start anywhere, at anytime, and persist. Stop worrying what others think about what you can or can't do. Believe in yourself and your abilities. Have the self-confidence to challenge your current situation. This is your life to live; it's day by day and step by step.

Write down your goals. Only three percent of people have written goals and only one percent review those written goals daily. Be in that elite one percent. Visualize the attainment of your goals often. Goals are dreams with dates attached. You will only become as great as the goals you choose. Think BIG.

2
Divide and Conquer

Break down any large task into a series of small tasks and start taking action. In the beginning, don't be too concerned with how you will achieve your goals. With commitment, research and patience, the means will come. Answers materialize when the facts have been collected. Your goals will evolve into a set of action-oriented objectives, which will become a series of to-dos. Every day, do what's on your to-do list. You will reach the objectives and eventually obtain the goal.

∼3∼

Write a Personal Mission Statement

Create for yourself an evolving document that outlines your purpose in life. Who are you? What are your values? What do you intend to do with your time to make your one life meaningful? Excepting acts of God, it is you who determines your future. You don't have to listen to those who say you are too old, too young, too poor, too unattractive, too uneducated or the wrong color, gender or nationality. They are not speaking of someone following the Action Principles.

When you read inspirational passages in other books, magazines or newspapers, write them down or clip them out. Put everything together in a folder or box. This will serve as your motivational reserve and will help you create a personal mission statement.

Your mission statement only has to be a few sentences or paragraphs. Refer to your mission statement periodically and don't be afraid to change it as you grow. A mission statement will help you to establish a foundation upon which you can build your dreams and goals and from which will flow your objectives and daily to-do list.

4
Follow Through

Follow through to make sure that you've done the job right. Follow through to say thank you and offer new ideas. Follow through to ask for more business. You build respect by saying what you're prepared to do and then doing exactly that. Follow through shows that you are a person of your word and someone who cares. It shows that you are accessible and that you want to keep the lines of communication open. You may make mistakes and follow through gives you the opportunity to correct and to learn from those mistakes. Personalize your follow-up with handwritten notes and phone calls. Small gifts, tickets and lunches may also be appropriate follow-up incentives. Check up on yourself and reap the rewards. Follow through amplifies your effectiveness.

⨾5⨾

Focus on Your Priorities

You could be doing a million things but you should pick one. What is the one most important thing that you want to do today, this week or this year? This is a common denominator among the successful. They are focused on the immediate accomplishment of specific objectives. Separate the important from the urgent and allow time for both. What must you do? What should you do? What would you like to do?

If you don't prioritize your day's activities, everything is of equal importance. Whether one thing gets done or doesn't get done may not matter. You want your activities to be important. Write your to-do list every day. Prioritize it. You want to feel a sense of accomplishment often.

~9 6 &~

Don't Complicate Matters

Don't complicate your life. Think before you act. Look for the simple ways or answers first. Make sure that you understand the assignment or the problem before you begin. What are the time and performance expectations that will indicate satisfactory completion? Reexamine how you are doing things. Is a task consuming all of your time? Is it worth the time you are investing? Can it be delegated? If so, is the right person assigned to complete the job? Your research, your quiet time, your commitment to teamwork and your prioritized to-do list should all help. Pare away the unnecessary. Even the philosophy underlying these Action Principles can be very simply put. Improve yourself and help others.

7

Commit to Never Ending Improvement

Every day look at your work and ask yourself how you can be more efficient and more effective and provide the highest quality service. Constantly seek ways to do things better in all areas of your life. The Japanese have a word for the concept of never ending improvement, kaizen. Progress and ultimate success come to those who train and keep training.

Measure yourself against the best. Most others will choose to be average. This is what average means. You won't know your limits if you don't keep trying. Reject the idea of good enough. Commit to excellence. Take each of your goals and think of how you can improve one percent each month. Success is a journey. It is not a quick fix. The joy is in the doing. Think of success not as a peak to be climbed but a high plateau to be walked.

Always encourage children or employees to do their best and to keep going. Set the bar high for yourself and them. You will all be the better for it.

≈ 8 ≈
Be Frugal

Separate your wants from your needs. You want to work for all you need, not necessarily for all you want. You do not have to sentence yourself to a lifetime of hard labor for the false trappings of status. Living on less can eventually yield much more. The simpler you make your life, the easier it will be to maintain. Think in terms of moderation. You can make a comfortable life for yourself by finding contentment in the things you already have and holding reasonable expectations.

Be pragmatic. To build an investment bankroll, you can work more or you can spend less. Many people who write and stick to a household budget find that the simple act of thinking and organizing before spending can yield savings of between 10% - 15% of their earnings without seriously compromising their lifestyles. Fewer than 25% of American households have stocks or mutual funds. Fewer than 3.4% have bonds. Only 8.4% have rental properties. Be frugal and be the exception.

∾ 9 ∾
Make Today Special

Many people enjoy using the first few minutes of the day for their reflective time. How did yesterday go? What do you want to accomplish today? What will be most important? This, of course, becomes your prioritized to-do list. How will today vary from your usual routine? Can you think of any small things that you can do? Perhaps there is something that you've been avoiding, that, if you do it, would make you feel especially proud of yourself.

Give each day a specific purpose. For unsuccessful, unhappy people, there is often a sameness to their days. Is it Monday or Thursday? Is it March or November? Is it 3 o'clock in the afternoon or 10 o'clock in the morning? They're in a rut and it doesn't matter.

Everybody has the same amount of time each day. How are you going to spend your 24 hours? Plan in advance. Make lists. Lists are your road map to personal accomplishment and balanced living. Always carry paper and pen. What are you doing today to ensure a better tomorrow for yourself and your family?

~9 *10* ᔐ
Record Your Thoughts

Carry index cards, a hand-held computer or a small notebook. You could borrow napkins to write on. As you become an action-oriented person, positive thoughts will occur with increasing regularity. Write down your ideas. You will have good ideas because you will have many ideas. Review your notes before your quiet time or before bed. You will become your own best therapist. You will see the ways to solving your own problems, finding your own route to happiness and realizing your own dreams. Spend most of your time thinking about solutions and not problems. Get back to recording your thoughts.

≫ *11* ≪
Use the Power of Patience

You can handle most problems because you know that only a little time stands between you and your goal. It may take twenty calls to make a sale. Be patient. It might take you five attempts to quit smoking or lose weight. It might take ten applications to get the job you really want. The point is that you try and keep trying until you succeed. Most people quit too soon. Be persistent. Be patient. Concentrate on your major goal until you have achieved it. It is not what you did yesterday. It is not what you may be doing today. It is what you are prepared to do every day.

Remember that all wealth, all businesses, all real estate and all treasures eventually pass from old hands to young. Be prepared. Your time is coming.

～12～
Maintain A Positive Attitude

A positive mental attitude results from having a balanced life plan reinforced by a daily commitment to self-improvement and service. Now, get up, stretch and be happy because today you are one day closer to your goals. You know who you are and where you are going. You are generous and kind and hard working. Above all, you are self-reliant. You know that success can be yours because success is in your own hands. You feel the enlivening power of having control over your own future. You expect good things to happen. Optimism is a wonderful feeling.

You are your thoughts. You are thankful for being tough enough to take a few setbacks and keep going forward. You are thankful to have the curiosity to keep learning. You are grateful to see opportunity knock so often. You are thankful to have the personality to keep making new friends. Your mind can only hold one thought at a time so make that one thought positive. Count your blessings. The way is clear. The world is a better place because you are in it.

∾ 13 ∾
Seize the Moment

Be ready. There is no better time to start taking positive action than right now. You can't change yesterday but you can build today for tomorrow. You research and seek advice while realizing that a time comes when you must act. Don't procrastinate. Work now. Enjoy now. Be mindful and in the present when you are washing the dishes. Be mindful and in the present when you are listening to your children.

When you feel that you should change a bad habit, seize the moment and do it. You must confront before you can change. When you feel like exercising, seize the moment. When you feel like finally doing something that you have been putting off, do it. If you can help someone out, do it. If you can start practicing a new skill, now is the time. Fully participate in the present. Don't worry about the past or future. Live now.

~ 14 ~

Act Independently

You are a person of action. You assess a situation and, based on your knowledge and experience, you act. You dare. You risk. You make mistakes. You reevaluate. You act again.

Because the status quo is often comfortable and safe, many people look for guarantees before taking independent action. Yet, in seeking assurances, they frequently receive cautions, which can easily be used as excuses for inaction. Those who love you the most may be the loudest in warning you not to risk.

If you always follow the crowd, you will always end up where the crowd ends up. You will never become a black belt if you think you look foolish wearing a karate uniform.

Make a personal decision to do what it will take to succeed. These principles are known to many but lived by few. Most people know what they should be doing. They lack the will or the self-confidence to test themselves physically and mentally by starting a business, making an investment or establishing a friendship. This is not the independent you. You are a person of action.

∽ 15 ∾
Cause Change

For there to be growth, there must be change. Since you seek growth, you must seek change. You must see yourself and your environment not only as it is but also as it could and should be. You seek the changes necessary to reach the better you so that you can play your part in making a better world.

First, you change yourself. Can you change your day and spend more time with your family? Can you change your standard lunch routine and take a walk? Can you change your drive home and stop at a nursing home for twenty minutes and see someone who may have few visitors? Can you change your office habits and find the time to make five more phone calls? What are the possible consequences of not changing?

≈ *16* ≈
Let Them Be

You don't have to apologize if all of your students or employees don't work to their potential. This is their choice. You are not obligated to pamper everyone all the time. Each student or employee will make an individual decision on whether to learn, to practice or work. Or, with their own free will, they may decide to take a different road. You can encourage but you can't force your views on people who won't help themselves or look ahead. In the face of threats or sarcasm or apathy, you may have to walk silently away. Sometimes taking a firm stand and issuing reprimands are necessary.

Every soldier can not be a Green Beret. Everyone who starts a job won't become a manager. Every student is not appropriate for advanced placement classes. Doing your best as a teacher or supervisor is enough. Help those who need help. You should not feel compelled to lower your standards to accommodate everyone.

≈9 17 ℰ
Accept Differences

See each person as an individual and not as part of a group. All humans from all countries and cultures are equal without regard to race, color, creed or gender. Believe with confidence and trust that the vast majority of people whom you meet, befriend or do business with are more similar than different from you.

People are inherently good. Most people act in good faith. They mean you no harm and would assist you in time of need. Don't waste your time thinking otherwise. Do not become a party to rumor or gossip.

Reject stereotypes and the divisive and demeaning policies that group people into categories.

~9 18 e~
Fail, Learn, Move On

Mistakes and failures are stepping-stones on the path to achievement. Failures can light the way to success. Nobody who challenges the status quo wins them all. When you are wrong, the most expedient form of action is to admit your mistake, learn from it and move on. All self-made businesspeople started small, made a lot of mistakes and built on the insights learned through hard work and continuing research. When they began, their ideas and goals may have seemed foolish and unrealistic, but they persisted.

Be prudent. Perhaps the smartest course of action is to retreat and reflect upon your options. Just because you deserve victory doesn't mean that you will win every fight, game or argument. Someone else may have the tactical advantage. Have the self-confidence to know when not to fight. The non-action of the wise man is not inaction. It is not studied. It is not shaken by anything. The heart of the wise man is tranquil. It is the mirror of heaven and earth ... emptiness, stillness and tranquility. Wise men don't fight each other.

~ 19 ~

Spread Your Enthusiasm

Putting the Action Principles to work in your life will elevate your soul and lift your spirit. You will feel a zest for life. You will live full, enriched days. This will happen because you will have taken the quiet time to think, organize and prioritize your days. You will love many things and these things will become part of your day. You will be in control. Every day you will do good things for yourself and others. Words like boring, bland and uneventful will rarely describe your work or your relationships.

Listen to your favorite CD. Call a friend. Read a good book. Smile. Hear. See. Feel. Smell. Take a walk and look at all the wonders of your world. Let everyone in your life know that life is worth living.

Be known as a motivator. Ask others about their goals and how you can help them. Make people feel part of a successful team. Solicit their input. Keep everyone informed and involved. Establish performance incentives. Look for opportunities to praise and reward. Enthusiasm is contagious.

≈ 20 ≈
Applaud the Beginner

You walk into a karate school for a first visit and see kicking, punching, blocking, chopping and flipping. It can be intimidating if you've never done these things. Or, you may look and feel awkward learning to snow ski or rollerblade or taking a foreign language. But persist; this is your first day and there will never be another first day.

Any new endeavor may be tough in the beginning. Accept this. You must believe in yourself. Some of your loudest critics may be those closest to you. When you ultimately succeed, everyone will claim to have been on your team from the beginning. Take action and persist. Applaud those who try, because the first step is often the toughest. Welcome the newcomer.

~ 21 ~

Give Yourself the Gift of Self-Reliance

If there is one gift that you can give yourself that will enhance the overall quality of your life, it is self-reliance. You already possess everything you will need to succeed. You can work on your own schedule toward your own goals without feeling pressured by the demands of others.

When you are self-reliant, if you lose your job, you'll get another. If you lose that job, you'll start your own business. You can make more money as a self-employed handyman applying the Action Principles to your work than a lazy lawyer will ever earn. You need the will, the self-confidence and a realistic plan. As a follower of the Action Principles, you will have them. Life just can't get you down because you are in control of yourself.

≈ 22 ≈
Lead by Example

Suppose you woke up tomorrow and you were the ideal you. Would you be: more daring, more powerful, more friendly, more accepting, more ambitious, more appealing, and more giving? Start acting immediately as the person you will be, a person of character with a sound reputation. Your words, your manner, your attitude, your dress, your posture and your actions are all reflections.

In modern society, people are constantly bombarded with visual and auditory messages. People need cues to sort good from bad and to find order so that they can make decisions. In many different aspects of your daily life, you are giving off cues that can be positive or negative. If you speak well, dress appropriately, smile, are courteous, work hard, volunteer and don't complain, you give people short cuts to view you in your best light. Your values and ideals have been deeply considered. You guide yourself and others toward excellence, not perfection. You are always open to new ideas, suggestions and offers of assistance. You must never ask or expect others to do what you would not do. You must be fair, firm, friendly and dependable. If you have to correct someone, do it in private.

You have succeeded as a leader when your team works just as well in your absence. Be constantly on the lookout for heroes in your own life to admire and emulate. Adopt their styles. Then, lead by example.

∼ 23 ∼

Control Conflict

Remain calm and detached. Allow others to rage while you consider the appropriate response. Should you reason, agree, apologize, fight or leave? Which is to your benefit and to the benefit of those you must protect?

Arguing often makes the other party become more defensive and determined to prevail. Let go of your anger. It only clouds the issue and draws you into a quick response. Temper anger with kindness. Kindness is a weapon against evil. Neutralize shouting with soft words. Answer threats with serene confidence. Speak plainly. Don't use foul language or sarcasm. Breathe deeply with long exhalations. Let the anger wash over you. Maintain your presence. Don't exaggerate. Don't lie. Attack the argument and not the person.

Long term relationships are almost always more important than short-term problems. Be an active peacemaker, building bridges of understanding.

≈ 24 ≈
Listen to Your Instincts

"I don't feel comfortable here. I don't like the sound of this. This doesn't look right to me."

With regard to your body or surroundings, your instincts are your best early warning system. Listen to the inner voice. Listen to that gut feeling. Go to the doctor. Leave the party. Get away from these people. Quit this job. Don't open that door. Duck into that store. The world is an imperfect place. There are dangerous places and people.

Every once in a while, your instincts may be off and you may feel foolish. Err on the side of safety and your instincts may save you from danger. Give yourself time or space to consider your options. It is foolhardy to do otherwise.

∾ 25 ∾
Face Fear

Knowledge, practice and courage are your weapons against fear.

One person can step out of an airplane door at 2,000 feet without hesitation. Another can stand before an audience of 2,000 and give a speech without breaking into a sweat. Fears can be rational or irrational but they are always personal and real. Everyone fears something.

To diminish a fear, you must first face it. The one hundredth skydive or speech won't be as traumatic as the first. The best way to deal with first fears is through a combination of logic and bravery. Logically, most people who jump from planes or give speeches don't die. They succeed through preparation. If your equipment is right and your training is complete, you are ready to jump. If your speech is carefully crafted and practiced, you are ready to speak.

Associate with confident people. You have seen many who have already done what you fear doing. Now, do what they have done. Courage grows with action. Fear is learned and must be unlearned. After facing that fear, you will feel exhilarated. Without fear, there can be no courage. Fear provides the opportunity to be brave.

~ 26 ~

Don't Be A Perfectionist

Trying to be perfect takes too much time and effort. It creates too much stress and is impossible anyway. Instead, strive to relax at the 90% level. This is the personal mastery level. Following the Action Principles, reaching the 90% level in most of your financial and social endeavors will be something that you don't even have to think about. It will happen through your persistence, determination, hard work and nice personality.

Right now, learn about the income and the lifestyle level of those in the top 10% of your profession. If you aren't content earning more than 90% of your co-workers, choose another profession.

It is possible to try too hard in business, exercise and relationships. Overwork can produce stress and anxiety which is the opposite of the inner peace you seek. Your best is good enough. Live to a high standard, not to an impossible obsession.

~∂ 27 ∂~
Remain Adaptable

In daily life, through a love of many things, it is possible to remain adaptable. If it starts raining on the way to the beach, you'll enjoy going to the movies. If you are kept waiting for an appointment, don't get angry. Make a few calls or work on your schedule. If you get stuck in traffic, enjoy your favorite motivational audiotape, radio station or CD. Always have a book with you and you will never be alone. The small stuff can't get you down if you are ready to substitute one good thing for another.

≈ 28 ≈

Think Win-Win

Thinking win-win is a frame of mind that seeks mutual benefit and is based on mutual respect. It is about bargaining fairly, and being open-minded and reasonable to all parties. It is about compromise and a sincere desire to find agreements that occupy the middle ground. Win-win is not taking advantage when it is understood that you are being trusted to act with honor.

It's about thinking in terms of abundance. There is an ever-expanding 'pie', a cornucopia of opportunity, wealth, and resources, not scarcity and adversarial competition.

❧ 29 ❧

Be Proud

Take pride in who you are and in those values and beliefs for which you stand. Be proud of your education, work and personal accomplishments. Be proud of your spouse, children and extended family. Be proud of your home and neighborhood. Be proud of your military. Be proud of your body, personal grooming and your manners. Be proud of the sports teams and cultural organizations that you support. Be proud of your public officials.

Don't be afraid of who you are, since you act with courage and compassion. Tell others, and bask in the feeling of being your best. Teach others, so they, too, may be proud.

∽ 30 ∾

Be Decisive

You don't have to wait for permission to do the right thing. Be decisive. Take the initiative. Get the facts. Do it now. If you don't have time to send a letter to a sick friend, send a card, a fax or an e-mail. If you can't visit your mother, call her. If you see a gift that a friend would love, buy it for him or her. If you can't go to the gym or dojo for ninety minutes, go for forty minutes.

Avoid not doing things because you can't get them done exactly as you'd originally planned. Be bold and get in the habit of doing something. Walk down one block. Pay three bills. Spend fifteen minutes with your children's homework. Give five dollars to charity. Small efforts done continually can yield significant, positive results. Do it now while it's on your mind.

To be happy, you don't have to wait to finish school, find a life partner, start a new job, lose weight, buy a new car or retire. Happiness is a journey and not a destination.

You don't have to be perfect to live the Action Principles. Just be a person of action. You must have more than good intentions to succeed. You must act. Get it done. Start it now.

≈ *31* ≈

Be the Warrior

The warrior is tough in loyalty, intensity, determination, bearing, initiative, endurance, courage and strength of will. The warrior is soft in calmness, self-confidence and compassion. The warrior is frequently called upon to step forward when most gladly step back. Warriors exist on the battlefield and in daily life.

People may react to you rudely, selfishly and with malice. Be courteous anyway.

Those you help may whine and offer no thanks. Help them anyway.

Your honest words may be challenged and ridiculed. Speak anyway.

Success may involve many mistakes and disappointments. Succeed anyway.

Your donations may seem too small to matter. Give anyway.

A warrior is a master, ever prepared to improve and to be of service to others.

∾ 32 ∾
Embody Integrity

As a follower of the Action Principles, you are proud, strong, friendly, generous and successful. Many will seek your counsel. People will depend on you. Have faith and a belief in your cause. Know what you will fight for and what you won't. Do not compromise what is right. Stick to your convictions and principles as you allow your ethical values to direct your decision-making. Integrity goes beyond self-interest to moral courage.

Keep your promises. Fulfill your commitments. People want to know where you stand and for what you stand. People respect honesty and sincerity, but hate hypocrisy. Be consistent. Speak in clear precise facts. Do what you talk. You cannot speak stronger words than, *"I give you my word."*

~৯ 33 ৫~

Stay Centered

In the battles of life, you will take punches. Some may hurt. This too will pass. You are the center of your universe. Take care of your own needs first. Then go to your family, then to friends, neighbors and employees. Move on to the larger communities. Don't use saving the world as an excuse to forget your family. Don't allow others to rush or pressure you to act before you can decide what is right. The most important thing that a father can do for his children is to love their mother.

Stand with your knees slightly bent. Head up. Breathe deeply from your belly. You are a very small part of the grand scheme of things. You are one with the universe. You are everything and nothing. Remain calm, balanced and aware.

≈ 34 ≈
Love Many Things

You proportionally increase your chances for happiness by increasing the number of things that you love doing. Love many things and your happiness will escalate into an enthusiasm for life, which will have a positive effect on you and those around you. Seek and enjoy those things that give your life value and purpose.

To love many things, you must be adventurous. Try new things. Be excited and passionate about life. Feel good. You must be able to see beauty in the grand scheme of things as well as in details.

Discover: music, art, books, food, T'ai Chi, karate, theater, travel, movies, sunsets, exercise, friends, gardens and the Internet. Open your mind. Find your preferences. Make your home, office and dojo beautiful places to love. Keep going...

Remember how lucky you are to have so many interests. Happiness may not be a result of financial success. Happiness is a result of loving many things and appreciating what you already have.

∾ 35 ⌒

Forget Everybody

Not everybody wants to do business with you. Not everybody wants to be your friend. Not everybody wants world peace. Not everybody wants to work hard. Not everybody wants to be president.

Not everybody is smart enough to be a rocket scientist. Not everybody is fast enough to run in the Olympics. Who is helped by pretending otherwise?

Trying to accommodate everybody is a trap. It can't be done. Be yourself. People know their own problems better than you do. Not everybody will listen to reason or even act in his or her own best interest. You can.

❧ 36 ☙
Maintain Your Presence

Your contented presence shows an air of simple elegance and refinement in attitude and form. You appear physically, emotionally and spiritually strong, yet you seem to have even greater strength in reserve. You are poised, coordinated and balanced. You command with effortless assured confidence. Be calm. Be deliberate. Feel assured and alert. Look good. Feel good. Keep your head up and your shoulders back. Keep your eyes forward. Breathe deeply. Speak with a soft voice in a thoughtful manner. Rarely interrupt. Be brief. Walk with a purpose. Don't rush. Have a firm handshake. Your eyes are friendly. Your demeanor is respectful. Let your smile begin in your mind. You exhibit both style and class.

The things you want drawn to you will come as a result of your good nature and determined persistence. Pause and savor the moment. Begin your work.

∽ઉ 37 ৎ∾
Act as You Feel

When you feel in the mood to do something, this is the best time to do it.

If you feel happy, smile.
If you feel daring, act.
If you receive good service, compliment.
If you feel energetic, do something positive.
If you know a good joke, tell it.
If you feel generous, give.
If you are interested in getting wealthy, save and invest.
If someone needs help, lend them your strong hands or soft voice.
If you give your word, keep it.
If you want to make things better, vote.

~9 *38* &~

Appreciate Your Appeal

Following the Action Principles makes you an appealing, charismatic person. Students will want to learn from you, bosses to promote you, banks to lend you money and customers to buy your products or services.

Your allure will be your genuine selflessness in wanting to help them to achieve their objective, whether it is to become a black belt or buy a car. By not trying to be a salesperson, but a true customer service person, you will make more sales. Charisma isn't painted on the outside. It comes from the inside. Be honest. Be yourself. Adopt this attitude and you will be liked by many – immediately.

~9 39 ~

Develop Your Sense of Humor

In all areas of life, a quick wit, a hearty laugh, a smile and a warm sense of humor are appreciated. To be a good joke teller, tell jokes often. Practice. Model your delivery after comedians you admire and funny friends. Start a joke file.

Always be absolutely sure that your material is clean and non-offensive. Stick to a universally funny subject – you. Most of the best humor is self-deprecating. That is, you have to learn to laugh at yourself. On your road to success, there will be many stumbles and fumbles, providing many opportunities for you to turn the unexpected into stress-reducing laughter. Don't sweat the small stuff. Laugh about it. Be affable. Humor will add to your attractiveness.

∼ 40 ∼
Become Grateful

Life isn't exactly the way you want it to be. You will have your ups and downs and crosses to bear. You will have opportunities to practice holding your tongue and exercising patience. Yet, because you are focused on the larger picture, you will be able to keep everyday events in perspective.

Be grateful for all you have. Acknowledge and accept compliments. In the larger scheme of things, you may wish to be grateful for good health, a supportive spouse, a rewarding profession, obedient healthy children, conscientious employees, prosperity, religious faith, loyal friends and even winning sports teams. You add and choose. Why not write letters to people in your life who have made a difference and thank them? You will both feel good.

When you can look forward and be thankful, you can help others do the same. Hold the burning candle from which others can light their candles.

Embrace gratitude.

≈⋑ 41 ⋐≈
Show Loyalty

Be a stand-up person. You stand for your family, country and friends. When and if trouble comes, let others have no doubt that they can count on you for help and support. Your commitments don't waiver with the moods of the moment. You don't hesitate to act.

At work, you build customer loyalty by concentrating on service with an attitude clear to everyone that customer retention is very important to you. You don't run a business solely dependent on finding new customers.

You are consistent, devoted, faithful and true. You stand for your beliefs and values. You aren't afraid to pledge allegiance to what is right. This is loyalty.

～42～
Practice Forgiveness

Anger, hatred, bitterness, resentments and thoughts of revenge are heavy weights that slow a person down. Allowed to fester, these negative feelings can consume increasingly larger portions of your life. Liberate yourself. Let it go. The forgiving person is always stronger. Be like the rock in the stream and let the thoughts of revenge flow by you.

As a person of action, improving yourself and helping others, you will make lots of mistakes. You will do foolish things. Learn the lesson.

You practice forgiveness for yourself. Consider those whom you may have offended or injured and ask for their forgiveness. Can you say, *"I'm sorry and I apologize if I offended you."*? If you ask and your request is rejected, you have lightened your burden in trying. Continue to encourage efforts at reconciliation.

∾ 43 ∾
Demonstrate Your Love

From the Bible, we learn that love is patient and kind. It does not envy. It does not boast. It is not proud. It is not rude; it is not self-seeking; it is not easily angered; it keeps no record of wrongs. It always protects, always trusts, always hopes, always perseveres. It is responsibility and a willingness to work out problems.

Love is too wonderful and too powerful to be kept bottled up. Let it out with your smiles, your voice, your manner, your enthusiasm and your continuing acts of kindness. For love, you can risk being vulnerable.

When you find love, cherish and safeguard it. A loving marriage and family is worth all your efforts.

~ 44 ~

Look Forward to Tomorrow

You can begin immediately to be the person you aspire to be. You don't have to wait. Do not be ruled by yesterday. In fact, change is often easy. The hard part is to maintain that change for the long term.

Hope does spring eternal. If you fall down today, you have tomorrow. If you fall down tomorrow, you still have the day after tomorrow. Keep at it. You will either succeed or end up being the toughest opponent most will ever meet. Everything starts happening right now!

～ 45 ～
Develop Your Special Talent

You were born with a special talent. It may be to sing, write, teach, paint, mentor, preach, defend or befriend. You have something special to offer the world, something you can do better than 10,000 others. You must keep learning and trying new things to find your special talent. The world needs your gift. Be aware that even a special talent can go stale if you don't keep using and honing it. Endeavor to keep your talents and all your skills up to date.

An advantage isn't an advantage unless you use it. Find ways to use your advantages to set and reach your goals. Likewise, you should recognize and then try to minimize the impact of your limitations. Remember that not all advantages are transferable. Just because you are talented in one area doesn't mean that you will be talented at everything you try. The successful real estate investor can easily lose her money opening a restaurant. Stick to your advantages and don't stray from them without reasoned justification.

❧ 46 ❧

Be Persistent

Modern life can make you soft. The status quo may become comfortably familiar. You can actually begin to believe that you are doing all that you can or that doing more isn't worth the effort. Challenge yourself. You must start the positive momentum in your life and then you've got to stick with it day to day.

You don't need someone else to tell you not to smoke. If today, you smoked a pack, tomorrow smoke 18. The next day, 17. Improve. If you haven't read a book recently, read one. If you don't exercise, take a walk around the block. If you're shy, say to five new people: *"Good morning!"*

You know yourself. You know what improvement you need. You don't need anyone to tell you not to jump from a fifty-story building, so why would you need someone to tell you not to do drugs, to exercise more, eat a sensible diet, talk to your kids, or compliment your employees? You know what to do.

Keep going. No one can say that you failed until you do. Keep taking small steps toward your goal. Challenge the you who is content with yesterday's accomplishments. Take a deep breath. Changes that last a lifetime begin in a moment. With persistence, only time stands between you and your goal.

～ 47 ～
Develop Winning Habits

If becoming a success were easy, everyone would do it. It isn't. They don't. As a follower of the Action Principles, you can. You can develop winning habits while identifying and working to eliminate your bad habits. Be patient. Psychological studies have shown that it takes between 21 and 28 days to begin to form or begin to rid yourself of a habit.

You can keep your word even though this may not always be easy. You can write and focus on your goals and objectives and your to-do list. You can exercise when you're tired. You can read business materials. You can volunteer. You can give a little extra money to charity. You can give a little extra time to family members, students and customers. You can pick up litter on the jogging path. You can delay gratification. You can do a lot while others are idle.

You won't always want to do these things. You will feel that you are doing more than your share. You are right. Work on your habits. You are tough.

❧ 48 ❧

Do What Others Can't

Most people can't give two nights a month to volunteer at a hospice. You can.

Most people can't get up at 6:00 AM and jog two miles. You can.

Most people can't give up half of their lunch hour to solve a customer's problem. You can.

Most people can't help to clean up other people's messes. You can.

Most people can't help a friend deal with destructive behavior. You can.

Most people can't give five percent of their money to charity. You can.

You are following the Action Principles.

$\approx$ 49 $\ll$

Accept Hard Work

Great accomplishments come from hard work. Luck accompanies hard work. If necessary, be prepared to endure temporary hardship. At times, the work is going to be hard to do and you would prefer doing something easier. Accept this. Put enthusiasm into your work and you will reduce boredom.

Your interest in learning will never wane. Your willingness to do for others will never disappear. Your commitment to high personal standards will not cease. Your dedication to the Action Principles won't stop. Commit yourself to hard work and be thankful that you aren't lazy. Laziness makes all work difficult.

From day one, you accept the premise that by following the Action Principles, you will work hard and give much. Don't cheat, or look for the easy way out. Bask in the feeling of exhilaration and accomplishment that few will experience. If you work hard, you will never go hungry. In the end, you will discover that all the hard work was worth it.

∾ 50 ∾
Venture Outside The Box

It would be nice if there were logical step-by-step instructions for every step on your success journey. But, there aren't. You learn from your own experiences and by studying the experiences of others, and then you often have to find your own way. To find an answer, you may have to go outside the box.

If all graphic designers are offering computer-generated work, maybe your niche is hand drawing. If all your day care center competitors are strict about pick-up times, maybe your niche is to be flexible. If none of the other landlords in your area allow pets, maybe you do. Being a little different can be profitable.

If you can't earn a degree full time, perhaps you can take evening or correspondence or on-line courses. If you are worried about starting a business, you can consider buying an existing business or a franchise. If you can't exercise because you have to baby-sit, how about taking the kids for a walk or run with you?

Don't give up. At times, you may have to improvise and get creative. Quitting or not trying isn't an option.

∼❦ 51 ❦∼

Communicate with Ease

Can you talk your way out of most tough situations? Can you talk your way through to decision makers to build up your sales? Can you talk to the media and garner positive press for your business? Can you talk to 500 people and win converts to your cause or position?

Being an effective communicator can take you a long way and is a skill worth developing. Be yourself. Believe in your own words. It doesn't matter if you are talking to one person or one thousand. If you want people to like what you say, persuade with modesty and build your audience up.

Listen to good communicators and model yourself after them. How do good interviewers ask questions? How do good public speakers work? How do good salespeople sell? To communicate well, you can't get stuck on transmit. Pause before you speak. You must listen and speak with purpose. Get to the point. Create interest with visual aids. Tell them what you are going to tell them. Tell them. Tell them what you told them. Sit down.

Don't let technology leave you behind. Learn to communicate via e-mail and the Internet.

≈ 52 ≈
Avoid Negative People

You have one life to live. You want to be happy and to make your life meaningful. You haven't got time to waste with negative people. They will drain your energy. When they find a willing audience, they won't let it go. They may have justifiable concerns but too often get over involved in minor matters. They blame and look for excuses. Even when blame can be justified it serves no productive good. They are usually negative because they have ceded control of their happiness to others – the boss, the neighbors, the kids, the politicians, the police.

Be polite and encouraging to negative people. You can be compassionate, but still be strong enough to walk away. Everyone has problems but not everyone allows those problems to rule them. You can offer a temporary safe haven without becoming a permanent home. You do not have to sacrifice your life to the problems of another.

~ 53 ~
Stay Fit and Healthy

Be prepared to succeed both physically and mentally. You do not know when you will be called upon to defend with a block, a blow or a word. You can swim, run, or rollerblade. You can take a walk. Staying fit also helps to prevent injury and helps you deal with stress and fatigue.

If you want to be thinner, start putting out more calories than you take in and you will lose weight. Start now. If you want to be healthier, add more fruits and vegetables to your diet. Drink a lot of water. If you want a strong heart, do twenty minutes of vigorous calisthenics each day. If you want to look good and feel strong, work out with weights three times a week for thirty minutes. You don't need fancy gym equipment to be fit. You don't need a lot of time. You just need the will to start and persist.

∽ 54 ∾
Relax Your Body

In your personal dealings, remain loose and light. Eliminate stress. There is rarely need to be tense and hardheaded. Much can be accomplished through calm reason and a soft voice.

Most physical movements should be loose, light, fluid, agile and flexible, rather than tense, hard, rigid or stiff. Slow, deep breathing will calm anxieties, lower your heart rate and allow for concentration. Massages, steam baths, saunas and whirlpools also help the muscles to rest. Make sure you get your rejuvenating 6-8 hours of sleep per night.

❧ 55 ❧

Invest In Your Future

Today, investors sacrifice and spenders enjoy. Tomorrow, investors enjoy and spenders keep working. If you buy a house today, you may have to work two jobs to make the mortgage payments now but you may own the house without debt in twenty years. If you give up TV tonight, you can take an evening course and in six years earn a college degree. If you start training today, you may be sore tomorrow and a black belt in four years. Invest in yourself.

Most wealthy people save between 15% and 20% of their income. Invest in fields in which you have a specialized knowledge. If you sell cars, invest in the auto industry. If you are a real estate broker, buy income properties. Be sure to diversify your holdings by investing in a retirement plan and a no-load mutual fund.

There is a time value to money, so the earlier you start investing the better. Invest in things that appreciate rather than spend on things that depreciate. Secure your own retirement and be sure that Social Security is the icing on your cake and not your whole cake.

～ 56 ～

Retire Early

If you didn't have to worry about earning a living, you could concentrate on your personal potential and being of service to others.

You don't have to be a millionaire to retire early. In fact, if you had savings of half that amount, invested prudently, you could retire and earn an annual income that exceeds the annual income of 75% of the people in the United States. Social Security should be a safety net or supplement and not the sole answer.

Over half of the people in the United States have less than $10,000 saved for retirement and live from paycheck to paycheck. They have no definitive financial plans. You are different. You now have a financial goal: to retire early.

Consider this: After 20 years of saving 20% of your income, you may create the choice of not having to work for a living.

Consider this: As an alternative to saving 20%, can you earn 20% more if you work 10 hours a day rather than 8, or 6 days a week rather than 5?

≈ 57 ≈

Have Faith

Look around the train, the classroom or the office and you will probably see ordinary people who are going to live ordinary lives. There is nothing wrong with this choice. But you feel differently. You read this book and you feel empowered. You go to MasterSuccess.com for more training. Your mind fills with ideas. You find mentors. You research. You dare. You persist. You make money. You save. You invest. You succeed. You put your free time and extra money to good use. Many around you could have done exactly the same thing. They didn't. You did. Why?

You can't easily answer this question. You must have faith. Thank God for making you extraordinary. Thank God for helping you see so many possibilities. Thank God for making you a person of action.

∞ 58 ∞

Follow Your Code of Honor

As a follower of the Action Principles, you adhere to a strict code of honor regarding your personal behavior. Your honor becomes your shield.

You do not need to prove your might at the expense of others.

You do not need diplomas, awards or the acclaim of others to know who you are.

You do not need an audience to do the right thing.

You do not need a lot of money or many physical possessions to be happy.

You do not need to stand first in line.

You do not need lessons to act civilly.

You do not need prompting to help someone in need.

❧ 59 ❧

Enjoy Quiet Time

Everyone needs quiet time in their day when they can just be with their own thoughts. This isn't daydreaming. The serenity of quiet time can be enjoyed in a variety of ways. It can be traditional Zen or transcendental meditation, but it can also be taking a walk, gardening, making a pot of tea or taking a long, hot shower. You may wish to pray. Each day, take twenty minutes to stop, reflect and enjoy being who you are. Think about the past, present, future or nothing in particular. Relax by yourself and you will feel renewed. Tranquillity will re-energize you. Without trying, you will be amazed at how your subconscious mind releases so many good ideas. As you reflect upon the true sense for your existence, you can better deal with hardships.

Just as the time you spend exercising strengthens the physical you, quiet reflection strengthens the spiritual you. Quiet time also gives you the opportunity to practice minding your own business. Take a deep breath and continue to breathe slowly and steadily. Look around. Use all your senses. You will find contentment in the solitude.

∾ 60 ∾
Look in the Mirror

Look at yourself as your family, co-workers, customers, students and the general public may be seeing you. Endeavor to like and admire what you and they see.

Don't kid yourself and fall victim to self-deception. You can't honestly judge others if you can't honestly judge yourself. You cannot build a stronger self if you rely upon what may be the self-serving false appraisal and expectations of others. Do yourself a favor and be honest with yourself. Are you doing all you can do? If you are not honest with yourself, doubts and fears will haunt you. During your quiet time each day, quickly contemplate the thought: Is this the way that I want to be thinking and acting? Make self-reflection a daily habit. Pay close attention to yourself.

⇌❁ 61 ❁⇋

Imagine

Imagine you can give your family all the money they need.

Imagine you can give your family all the time with you they need.

Imagine you will be seen as a respected leader in your community.

Imagine your students will like you.

Imagine your employees will work hard for you.

Imagine people are telling you that you are making a difference in their lives.

Imagine you can accomplish all you want.

This is not a daydream. This is a result of following the Action Principles.

❦ 62 ❧

Hold Sacred...

... your religious faith.
... your family.
... your good name.
... your given word.
... your moral code.
... your self-reliance.
... your positive attitude.
... your healthy lifestyle.
... your self-improvement.
... your love of learning.
... your willingness to share.

∾ *63* ∾

Be Honest With Yourself

Rely on your strengths. To know your strengths, you must first acknowledge and then compensate for your weaknesses. Ask your friends and mentors: What am I good at? In what areas should I improve? What do you do better than most people? Don't be afraid to ask for advice or help and don't be afraid to listen to the answers. Reflect and learn. Knowing yourself allows you to plan your days for peak performance.

In business, solicit comments on your products and services. Customer and employee compliments and complaints are important tools to improve efficiency. Who knows you better?

Accept your limitations. Accept your circumstances. Following the Action Principles, you should have more than enough of everything to succeed. Be the best you can be on the inside, and your beauty and confidence will be reflected on the outside.

～ 64 ～
Understand Courage

There is a difference between physical and moral courage. If you earn a black belt in karate, you may be called upon to be physically courageous but such events will be extraordinary. Even police officers, firemen and military personnel may only have to be physically courageous a few times in their careers.

Moral courage is needed more often than physical courage. Moral courage may mean the challenge to stay with a belief when your position may not be the most popular. Moral courage can be standing tall against bigotry, prejudice, unfairness, and bullying behavior. Moral courage is a challenge to do what is right regardless of the personal consequences. Moral courage may ask you to forgive.

Think of people in physical pain or mental anguish. You may see courage being lived every day.

~9 65 c~

Ask Yourself

Are you healthy enough to keep to a regular exercise schedule?

Are you self-disciplined enough to stick to your prioritized to-do list?

Are you smart enough to be able to debate current affairs?

Are you brave enough to take a moral stand?

Are you humble enough to ask for help?

Are you strong enough to delay material gratification?

Are you merciful enough to forgive those who offend you?

Are you generous enough to share your good fortune?

≈9 66 ⋐

Run the Short Road

The short road leads you to physical fitness. If you work out three or four times a week, in three to four months you will probably be in good shape. This is a short road to a notable accomplishment.

The short road leads to financial independence. If you offer a quality product or service and you appreciate your customer and you keep improving, you will earn enough money not to have to worry about it. This is a short road to a notable accomplishment.

The short road leads to strong personal relationships. If you smile at, listen to and are generous with family, employees and the public, you will be rewarded with many friends. If you are courteous, you will be welcomed anywhere. This is a short road to a notable accomplishment.

～ 67 ～

March the Long Road

On the long road, experience beats inexperience, smart beats uninformed, effort beats laziness; polite beats rude; generous beats selfish; fit beats fat and interested beats bored. Be patient. Your time is coming. With time, everything passes from old hands to young.

On the long road, time will reward the prudent investments you make today.

On the long road, you accept the physical, mental and financial blessings that you enjoy from following the Action Principles as you continue throughout your life to improve yourself and to give back to your family and society.

❧ 68 ❧

Close the Door on the Past

The past is only alive if you keep it alive. You can't change yesterday but you can build today for tomorrow. Don't shackle yourself with regrets. Don't start feeling sorry for yourself. Whatever your previous circumstances, others have gotten through the same or worse. Appreciate yourself as a tested survivor: strong and determined. Learn from the past but don't assume that your past automatically equals your future.

Instead, fill your life with anticipation. Set your goals. Write your to-dos. Just because you haven't done something before doesn't mean that you can't start doing it right now. Be the new dynamic you. Right now.

∼◦ 69 ◦∼

Avoid Thinking That ...

... you need to chant or fast to find yourself.
... you need a lot of money to start a business.
... you need more than eight hours sleep.
... you need a personal trainer to exercise.
... you need advanced university degrees to be successful.
... you need to work forty or fifty years before retirement.
... you need special physical abilities to become a black belt.
... you need more time or resources before helping others.
... the world owes you anything.

∼∾ 70 ᥱᥱ
Count the Time

How long does it take to exercise?

How long does it take to stay informed?

How long does it take to be well groomed?

How long does it take to read your child a bedtime story?

How long does it take to say a kind word or deliver a compliment?

How long does it take to clean up after a meal at a shelter?

How long does it take to complete the next entry on your to-do list?

How long does it take to vote?

Probably just minutes.

～ 71 ～
Act With Boldness

Everyone admires the bold, courageous and daring; no one honors the fainthearted, shy and timid. Look around at what others have done and what you can also do. Everyone is afraid. The strong act in spite of the fear. The weak cower because of the fear. Timidity breeds doubt and hesitation that not only weakens but can be dangerous. The coward dies a thousand deaths.

Careful planning is a must. Careful planning and practice build self-confidence and a resolute spirit. The opposite would be constantly second-guessing and endless opinion seeking. Believe in yourself and the thoughtful decisions you make. However, a time comes for action. Be bold. Take the step. If adjustments are needed, adjust. If mistakes are made, learn from them and try again.

≈ 72 ≈
Rejoice In the Day

You got up early. You did your best at work. You exercised your mind and body. You were pleasant to others. You did a good deed. You took time to reflect and plan tomorrow. Take pleasure in your accomplishments. Be proud of yourself. If you keep putting days like this together, there is no telling how far you will go and how many lives you will be able to touch in a positive way. Today, you moved one day closer to achieving your goals.

Celebrate small victories and small joys and small wonders. You did your best. Put your head on your pillow. Live vibrantly. Sleep peacefully.

73

Do What You Love Doing

There are 5,000 different types of occupations. Choose one that you love. People have been successful at all of them. They are your models. You can do the same. When you love your job, it doesn't seem like work. If you are caught in dead end employment, use your free time to find a job that you can love doing or start your own business.

There are unlimited activities to occupy your free time. Make sure that each of your days, weeks, months and years are full of activities that you love doing.

Plan to spend a lot of your time doing what you love. You are in control of your own happiness.

~ 74 ~

Appreciate Your Customers

It is people who are going to give you their time, help or money, so you can have everything that you ever wanted in your life for yourself and your family. Those people are voters and tenants and fans and customers and clients and patients. Listen to them. Appreciate them. They hold the keys to your success. By focusing on the needs of others, a wonderful thing happens. You get everything that you want. Customer service is important for the customer but it is essential to your business. Without customer service, you don't have customers and you don't have a business.

～♪ 75 ♪～
Build Networks

You can go a long way by yourself, but you advance much better, much faster, with the help of others. Seek out others with a common purpose and help each other. Work through your mentors. Find them. Tell them why you admire them. Successful people will not be threatened by your enthusiasm for success. Sincerely ask for their help and often you will be rewarded with positive suggestions and the names of contacts. Carry and exchange businesscards. Rehearse a personal introduction that clearly and precisely states who you are and what you do.

Form alliances for common purposes. Establish your own personal support systems. Where do you find good attorneys, physicians, investment advisors, dentists, tailors, or contractors? Ask those you respect for recommendations. If you have a computer, buy a contact management program, and as you meet new people, add them to your personal network database. Keep in regular contact with your network. Form your support systems and personal networks before you need them.

~9 76 e~
Build Your Team

In building your winning team for business success or a political campaign, don't be afraid to pick people who are stronger, faster, smarter, better organized, braver, more ambitious, funnier or more pleasant than you are. Ask your best people for recommendations. Always opt for quality. Quality is remembered long after price is forgotten.

Think about the spirit on the best teams you were ever on and how your teammates cooperated in reaching a common goal. Think about the dignity and respect your teammates showed to one another. Think about how you were able to rebound from losses to play and win again.

You want your team to be built on excellence. You want your team built with members of merit and character. Resist those who propose membership based upon patronage. Excellence is excellence and is not subject to conditions of race, color, creed, national origin, etc. If someone is the best-qualified person to fulfill the team's mission, then, that's what they are. If they are not, they are not.

~ 77 ~
Negotiate With Power

Research and prepare before you meet. Speak with quiet authority. Know what you want and will accept before you begin. Ask for what you want. You shouldn't expect the other party to guess what you want. Be sure that the person you are speaking with can grant your request. Be persistent. Try different angles of attack. Ask the other party to suggest a resolution. Suggest a compromise.

Start the negotiation process with a lower than expected offer. Be reasonable. Don't argue or threaten. Respect the other party's position. Suggest logical arguments for your request. Clearly state your opinion of repercussions to both parties if an agreement is not reached. When you finalize the sale or negotiate the deal, stop talking, shake hands and move-on to a neutral topic.

∼⊸ 78 ⊶∽
Give Freely

The single best word in advertising is free. So give freely and reap the rewards.

If you are a hairdresser and need new customers, don't sit in the salon doing nothing. Hand out business cards, give free haircuts and show your expertise.

If you are a black belt, offer free self-defense clinics at factories, schools, fairs and anywhere else that will let you.

If you are an artist, donate one afternoon a month to teaching at the children's hospital.

Look for ways to say, *"free"* and keep giving.

When you give with positive intent, you don't have to worry nor should you be worried about the benefits. You will feel good. You will feel appreciated.

There is a universal human law of reciprocity. When you give something to someone, that person feels obligated to give something back. It could be new business. It could be media attention. It could be a testimonial letter. It could be a heart-felt *"Thank you."*

≈ 79 ≈
Work At Work

Work expands to fill the time available. Many people will work only up to expectations. Some work just hard enough to not get fired. Some people actually work as little as possible at work. These people create a window of opportunity for you. Don't worry about being obligated to work more hours to beat the competition. You probably don't have to invest more time. Instead, if you work all the time you are at work, you will probably come out well ahead of your competition. Guard your time; discourage interruptions.

However, don't become lulled into mistaking activity for accomplishment. Follow your prioritized to-do list. Live and appreciate every day as an important day.

≈ *80* ≈

Learn

You are responsible for your own education. When you want to learn about a new subject, go to the library. Go to the bookstores and buy books and magazines. Log on to the Internet. Join a club or association. Find experts in the field. Ask questions and more questions. Take courses and ask your teacher questions. Don't just sit there. Make the course your course.

As you begin a new subject or reach a new plateau in your studies, there may be awkward and embarrassing moments. Don't be afraid or think that you lack the aptitude to succeed. Everyone goes through the same learning curves. Ask questions. The only dumb question is the one not asked. Work to understand the basics. Stick with it.

Hunger for knowledge, because knowledge is power. You don't need to attend famous universities, or burden yourself with piles of college tuition debt. You can learn anything you want to learn. It is a gift that you give yourself. Knowledge is portable. You take it with you everywhere. By our example, we must instill a love of learning and reading in our children.

～ 81 ～
Ask a Lot of Questions

The best way for you to learn about anything is to ask a lot of questions. Do not be shy. You want to be curious about a lot of new things. Questions are stepping-stones to self-improvement. The only meaningless question is the one not asked. To learn about politics, ask questions of the candidates. Dialogue will make you a better-informed voter.

In reverse, when you find yourself in the role of supervisor, be open and not intimidating. Solicit questions and suggestions. Dialogue will make you a better supervisor. Communicate with your staff, colleagues and constituents.

What does your staff need? Ask them often. What do your customers need? Ask them often. You need a satisfied staff to provide customer services and without satisfied customers, you are out of business.

≈◦ 82 ◦≈
Read Biographies

What if you could learn the success secrets of the greatest people who ever lived? You can.

The lives of the famous and the infamous have been recorded in biographies and are ready for you to read and research.

The lives of great government leaders, businesspeople and humanitarians are there. You will read about successes and triumphs. You will also learn how many times champions lose on their way to winning.

In reading biographies, you may come to the startling conclusion of how much greatness you possess. You may conclude, "Hey, I can do that." You can make your life significant. Biographies help show the way. You only have to take the action to go to the library, bookstores or surf the Internet.

❧ 83 ❧

Be Open to New Ideas

Your employees, family, friends, suppliers and even your competitors may all have suggestions that you can put to profitable use.

Be open to the fact that lots of people are going to have ideas worthy of your consideration. Welcome them. Incorporate the better ideas into your campaign, business and personal dealings.

Find new ideas in books, magazines, videos, audiotapes, newsletters, trade literature, and on the Internet. Find new ideas at conventions, seminars, lectures, and by taking evening courses. Find new ideas by networking at the Chamber of Commerce and at other professional and civic organizations.

We must guard against being unchangeable or apathetic.

∽ 84 ∽

Heed the Warnings

"High voltage." "Wear Your Seat Belt." "Capacity Limited to 150." "Danger - Thin Ice." "Don't Drive Drunk."

You may wish that you were invulnerable but you are not. You are human and your body can get hurt if you aren't a vigilant guardian of your own physical safety. Awful accidents may happen beyond your control. They are accidents and acts of God. But we are also often forewarned. A prudent person appreciates the warnings.

On occasion, you will find yourself in the company of stupid people who don't care about their own safety or yours. Be courageous. Speak up and then leave them to their stupidity.

∽ *85* ∾
Observe and Be Aware

At first, observation and awareness will require conscious effort on your part. Over time, it will become instinctive and will be one of your most valuable skills.

In business, you see ads and get ideas for your ads. You shop in stores and get ideas for your store. There is no point in re-inventing the wheel. If a proven strategy already exists, find it and try it.

In self-defense, you enter a movie theater and you make a mental note of the exits. You walk down an unfamiliar street and automatically scan for the unusual.

Listen to the speech patterns of powerful people. Be silent. Think twice and speak once. Be an active listener. Look at the person who is talking. Don't interrupt. Be aware of their body language. Listen and they will like you. Your self-confidence in mind and body will create a charismatic aura. Ask questions. Stay informed. Get involved. Read newspapers, magazines and books. Watch the news.

∼ 86 ✐

Read, Read, Read

There are few things that you can do that are more important than to instill a love of reading in your children. Reading is a lifelong gift. If you read, you can always educate yourself. It doesn't matter if you are reading from a computer screen, a paperback or from a leather-bound classic.

Set the reading example in your home. Keep plenty of books, magazines and newspapers in the house for everyone to read and discuss. Set family reading goals and provide children with incentives for reading. Set aside a time each week for reading aloud as a family. Take regular family trips to bookstores and libraries. Make sure children are involved in a summer reading program. Encourage all family members to give books as presents.

❧ 87 ❧

Respect and Defend All Life

Who will stand and speak for the children, for the condemned, for those depressed or suffering in physical pain? Defend the rights of the old, lonely, homeless, unwanted, forgotten, the harassed, physically and mentally challenged and depressed. Our blessings morally obligate us to share our time, money and expertise.

The easy course would be indifference and apathy reflected in our silence. When we do not fight for every life, we jeopardize our own. As the twenty-first century dawns, how many alternatives are we willing to consider before we give up even one life? Can we reach out compassionately to those dealing with life issues? Don't we have enough time, talent, money, and love to keep trying?

The strong and brave must defend those who cannot do this themselves. This is leadership. It is preserving human dignity and defending human rights. There, but for the grace of God, go I.

∾ 88 ∾

Honor Our Military

As we work toward world peace and we commit to finding nonviolent solutions to our problems, we must acknowledge that our freedom to do so has come as a direct result of those brave men and women who have served in our military. There is no doubt that without a strong response from good that evil would have triumphed. We must remain vigilant in our support of our armed services.

Once we begin to rely upon demoralized troops to fight push button wars, our security is jeopardized. Once we begin to believe that our defense can be left to others, we will soon be lost.

Right now, we can do more. In every city and town there are plaques and street signs to those who stood in our places to defend freedom. They left and did not return. They died heroes. They died for us. Yet, we have allowed their memories to fade. School children do not know their stories. We do not know their names. Can you adopt one fallen hero from your town and proclaim his or her name as a hero?

❦ 89 ❦

Treasure the Earth

We are obligated to future generations to protect our world. Clean air, clean water, green open spaces, national parks and preservation of our natural resources are everyone's business. Each of us can do our part. We can pick up litter in parks and streets without worrying how it got there. We can recycle and be aware of the disposability of the products we buy. We can plant trees. Educators and parents must join together to teach environmental awareness to our youngsters and, by example, the importance of conservation.

∽ 90 ∼
Allow Your Opponent To Save Face

In business, sport or everyday relations, always allow your opponent to save face. You won. That should be enough. Bragging is counterproductive – you simply present the opportunity for your audience to think the opposite. It costs little for you to offer your opponent the opportunity to excuse his loss. In fact, you may gain appreciation from many observers.

To taunt or shame a defeated opponent may simply set the stage for another confrontation, with the odds stacked against you. Your humiliated opponent may plot to redeem his lost honor by staging a rematch with more allies and more powerful weapons. You turn a quick battle into a long-term war.

If you lose, do so with grace and good spirit. You won't always win but you can always do what you believe to be right. For you, there will be another day. If you win, be gracious in victory because some day very soon you will be vulnerable. Winning provides you with the opportunity to show both mercy and humility.

~ 91 ~
Thank Your Ancestors

Learning is a process of self-discovery. Usually, that self-discovery is based on the trial and error and experience of those who have come before us. Someone ventured forth from the safe warmth of the prehistoric campfire. Someone hankered for a better life overseas. The curiosity and bravery of others has given us the knowledge to live long, comfortable lives. The human race is stronger and more adaptable today than ever before. Whatever you hope to accomplish with your life, the going will be easier because of the hard work and chances taken by those who came before us.

Be grateful for the explorers and scientists. Be grateful for soldiers who won our freedom. Be grateful for all teachers who pass the love and enthusiasm for their subjects to us. Be grateful to your parents. Be grateful to your personal mentors.

Continue down the path. Respect those who work on your behalf. Some day, you will be old and will appreciate the repayment of others' kindness. Thank your ancestors.

❧ 92 ❧
Practice Peace

Peace begins within each of us. We find it in our quiet time in personal reflection. It is shown in the understanding and forgiveness that we extend to each other. We can only teach peace by becoming examples of peace. Being peaceful, we extend peace to all we encounter. Peace is not a far away place but right here, right now.

Peace is not born from weakness. We must practice peace. As people of action, we must assume the mantle of defenders of the peace. We must remain vigilant and ready, willing and able to take the action to protect those in our neighborhoods victimized by bullies. Enemies of peace must never be appeased through our apathy or encouraged by our indecisiveness.

～9 93 ～

Make Everyone Feel Important

Teach with enthusiasm and your love for your subject will spread. Sell your products or services with enthusiasm and your company will grow. Presume that your students and employees and customers are your equal because they are. Don't teach or sell down to anyone. Speak with and not at or to your students or customers. Learn and use peoples' names.

Make everyone you meet feel important. You can't be selectively likable. If you try to like some people and not others, you will eventually be seen as a phony and no one wants to do business with a phony.

When you talk down to people, you shift the focus from your subject or product to your condescending attitude.

Listen. Be patient. Pay attention. Don't interrupt or fidget. Make eye contact. Smile and nod encouragement. Don't try to top another's story with your own heroic tales.

People love to be involved in projects which they helped design. Help others to identify and develop their strengths. Be quick to praise and slow to criticize. Look for opportunities to teach others about the Action Principles.

~ 94 ~

Give Generously

Follow the Action Principles and you will be blessed with much more than you need. You will work hard towards your goals and you will be liked. Just these two attributes will result in your being well rewarded. Your organizational abilities will allow you to have more time than most. Your persistence and determination will get you more financial reward than most. You must earn before you can give. Share your time and money. Send lots of flowers, candy, e-mails, handwritten cards, teddy bears and thank yous. Extend a helping hand. Smile. Compliment. Tell jokes. Laugh. Remember names, anniversaries and birthdays. Be generous and then forget it.

Selflessly, share your time and money because it is right. You will set in motion a chain of positive actions and reactions. To be unselfish, sharing, generous, bountiful, magnanimous, noble-minded and gracious is much more about attitude than about money. As much as you give, much more will you receive.

≈ 95 ≈

Share the Credit

If you organize a group to clean up a park, let everyone enjoy the thank yous. If your sports team wins a competition or makes a good showing, be proud, step back and let everyone walk around with the trophy.

If your sales team meets its objectives or if your customer service department solves a tough problem, take everyone out to lunch. Let everyone laugh.

As a leader, your greatest satisfaction should come from seeing the people in your team, department or company succeed. Share the credit and experience the camaraderie. You know who you are. Let others glow in the feeling of accomplishing a mutual goal. Be enthusiastic for others. Acknowledge exceptional work. Encourage cooperation. Your reward will be many friends.

Are we ready to say, *"Yes, we can do more. Yes, we can give more."*?

⮾ 96 ⮿

Promote Master Success

The Master Success System is yours. It is non-profit. Take from it what you need and add to it what you can. The surest way for you to stay on your personal journey to peace and prosperity is to get involved. All the work that you do for us helps others and reinforces your own commitment to success.

Take action. Spread the word and help us help others. You can tell co-workers and friends about the system. Send them to MasterSuccess.com to learn more. You can give a copy of this book to someone that you care about. You can check that the public and school libraries in your town have copies of the book. If you are able, purchase and donate copies of the book to social or educational organizations. You can start and participate in Master Success Groups in your area. Share your success and your knowledge.

～ 97 ～
Walk The Talk

When you live your life with concern and love for others, wonderful things will happen. You will be fulfilled. You will feel a warm pride from your selfless acts that will then allow you the grace of humility. To be first, you must put yourself last. The true leader goes to the end of the line. Say what you mean and mean what you say.

Can you give a dollar to a beggar? Can you lend an ear to one avoided by others? Can you work an extra shift for a parent who needs to be with a sick child? Can you visit a shut-in? Can you speak up and defend a poor soul being teased or bullied? Can you treat all people as your brothers and sisters? Your example may become contagious.

As Mother Teresa has taught us, the greatest sorrow is to be lonely and unloved. Refuse to let this happen with your idle consent.

Right now, the days of homelessness, hunger, and unsafe streets can be over if we make the commitment.

~ 98 ~

Teach Our Children...

... a respect for all life.

... the benefits of hard work, frugality, saving and investing.

... the value of physical fitness and healthy living.

... the merits of military and public service.

... the importance of charity and volunteering.

... a pride in heritage, home and country.

... the advantages of courtesy and manners.

... the power of knowledge.

... the blessings of positive thinking.

... the strength in self-reliance.

... the goodness of man.

... faith in God.

Children will only learn from us as we become the example.

≈ 99 ≈
Mentoring

If you want to learn first hand about a new subject and drastically shorten the learning curve, one of the best ways is to find a mentor. A mentor is an experienced person who is doing or has done what it is that you want to do and agrees to be your guide. Many successful people remember their own early struggles and gladly agree to serve as mentors, especially if you are an enthusiastic, appreciative novice. Besides sharing their knowledge, some mentors offer the additional bonus of sharing their contacts and networks. Imagine being able to consult with a senior partner who has been there and done that and whom you don't have to pay.

As others are willing to help you, don't forget your own potential role as mentor. This is what the Master Success System is all about; one person helping another who helps another. Even a small amount of time can make a big difference to a newcomer. Listen for the wise words of experience.

∞ 100 ∞

Call to Action

It is the people who make America great. Many of our ancestors came here poor and alone, some in chains. Yet, we have not only endured but thrived. In a few hundred years, we have achieved unheard-of gains, made the world safe for democracy and assumed the mantle of leadership. Now as individuals and as members of a greater community, we face great challenges to our schools, retirement and health care, military, environment and to the very moral values that have made us great.

We have done a lot. Guided by principle and faith in God, we can do so much more. This is a call to action. Following the Action Principles will show you the clear path to peace and prosperity in your life. Now, pass it on.

MASTER SUCCESS MAXIMS

A maxim is a general truth, fundamental principle, or rule of conduct. Do you have a Master Success Maxim that you'd like to share? Please add your maxim at MasterSuccess.com.

Adapted from the 100 Action Principles of the Master Success System

Start anywhere, at anytime, and persist.
Forgive quickly and move on.
Rid yourself of selfishness.
Help others for you and them.
Do it before you're asked.
Don't harm anyone.
Prepare to endure.
Think positively.
Celebrate self-reliance.
Ask and listen for the answers.
Tell jokes and have fun.
Commit to hard work.
Do more and want less.
Follow a principle-centered life.
Teach so others may have an easier journey.
Support the arts.
Find a way without excuses.
Treat others as you wish to be treated.
Speak once and listen twice.
Treasure a happy marriage and family.
Peace begins inside you.
Plan daily with prioritized to-dos.
Toughen your body and will.
Imagine the possibilities.
Submit to a high moral code.
Spread your enthusiasm.
Be morally courageous.
Do not compromise what is right.
Keep your promises.
Avoid self-destructive people.
Measure yourself against the best.
Count your blessings.
Change yourself first.
Strive to be happy.
Love many things.

Appreciate what you already have.
Improve yourself.
Read and learn anything.
Imitate your heroes.
Seek the support of others.
Make your word your bond.
Accept responsibility.
Pause and savor the moment.
Learn from your mistakes.
Display good manners.
Make every day special.
Build your character, not your reputation.
Do the important and not just the urgent.
Practice frugality; save and invest.
Reject stereotypes.
Seek humility and simplicity.
Always be protected.
Make everyone feel important.
Care about people more than things.
Defend the defenseless.
Renew your spirit through daily reflection.
Present yourself as an example.
Listen to your intuition.
Trust yourself.
Be known for your ethics and honesty.
Embody integrity.
Concentrate, focus and aim straight.
Say what you mean and do what you say.
Look for the simple answers first.
Separate your wants from your needs.
Be mindfully in the present.
Temper anger with kindness.
Applaud those who try.
Persist in doing good.

ACKNOWLEDGEMENTS

Many special people have directly blessed my life and kept me headed in the right direction on my personal journey to peace and prosperity. I thank all my teachers and the nuns and priests who have guided me. I thank my mother.

Karen is my wife. She has cleaned and painted apartments. In addition to the responsibilities of being an urban high school English teacher, she has patiently edited my writings on many long nights. For over a quarter of a century, she has put up with someone who is frequently shifting between being a martial arts instructor to real estate investor to business writer to motivational speaker. Enough can't be said.

Bill, Sr. is my father and a self-made man. It took me a long time to recognize and acknowledge his role in my success. He gave each of his children a hand when they needed a hand. He did something difficult. He relinquished control while giving us the support necessary to become independent.

Bob Unanue is a Director of ASI and my brother-in-law. His endorsement and backing of my ideas has allowed the American Success Institute to mature beyond its infancy. Any further success to a large extent will reflect Bob's personal efforts and continuing support.

Margaret Mary is my sister and a national leader in the field of higher education. Her encouragement and networking has been invaluable and has never flagged.

If you enjoy this book and our websites, you can thank my collaborators, Paul Watts and Kevin Maguire for their ideas, suggestions and technical expertise. The outstanding graphic work of Karen Watts has brought the American Success Institute national recognition for design excellence. Jessica Plachy, my assistant, works with a smile even when I am more often the hectic man of action rather than the calm man of peace.

I owe a debt to all my martial arts instructors. In particular, three Shaolin Kempo masters have supervised my martial arts training. They are John Fritz, Joan Richert and Mark Grupposo.

I would like to thank the friends of the American Success Institute for their continuing efforts including my friend Steve Rapson who has volunteered many days to many of my projects. I am also grateful for the friendship of Anne Carr, the musical talent of Ivo Weisner and the photography of Roger Barnaby.

Certificate of Achievement
AMERICAN SUCCESS INSTITUTE
This is to certify that
Jessica Plachy
has successfully completed the
Master Small Business course

Bill FitzPatrick
Executive Director

August 25, 1999
Date

THE MASTER
SMALL BUSINESS COURSE
online at

MASTERSUCCESS.com

This 30-lesson course traces the activities of three characters as they move from the idea of opening their own businesses until the day that they are able to turn the key to success. The course stresses the style and attitudes necessary to compete as an entrepreneur in the 21st century. Each lesson contains supplemental links to free educational materials available on the Internet. These materials cover all aspects of running a business. To continue your education, an extensive, annotated bibliography is included with each lesson.

If you've ever dreamed of owning your own business either full or part-time, this course should be near the top of your to-do list. If you already own your own business, this course can give you the ideas necessary to take your business to the next level. If you work for someone else, this course can make you a significantly more valuable employee.

Bonus. Following completion of the course and a short evaluation, you will be sent a Master Small Business Diploma suitable for display in your home or office.

Recommended time to complete: 3 – 4 hours per week for 15 weeks. For a FREE sample lesson, go to MasterSuccess.com.

Tuition: $197.

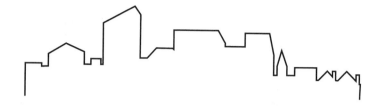

THE MASTER
REAL ESTATE COURSE

online at

MASTER*SUCCESS*.com

More money has been made in real estate than in all other industrial investments combined. With a reasonable amount of study, you can become a local real estate investment expert and gain considerable negotiating advantage. With a few successful part-time investments, you may be able to equal or exceed your full time income. This 30-lesson course covers all the important aspects of real estate investing. Particular attention is given to the style and attitudes that make successful real estate investors. The investment philosophies of America's greatest investors will be discussed. You will be taught not only how to spot profitable opportunities but how to create them. To supplement the course, you will be linked to hundreds of important real estate investment websites for further study and opportunity. An extensive annotated bibliography will accompany each lesson.

Recommended time to complete: 2 hours per week for 15 weeks.

For a FREE sample lesson, go to MasterSuccess.com.

Tuition: $197.

THE MASTER
SELF-DEFENSE COURSE

online at

MASTER*SUCCESS*.com

This is a three-part, 30-lesson self-defense course. In part one, lessons 1-20, the focus is on learning simple protection techniques to use quickly and effectively to safeguard you and those you love. What should you always do? What should you never do? You will learn how to stay safe at home, work, on vacation, and on public transportation. What should you always carry in your car, in your briefcase, pack or purse? What should you keep in your desk? The pros and cons and basics of using weapons are covered in this section. Learn from the best. Each lesson features an interview on self-defense with an expert.

In part two, lessons 21-25, you will gain an understanding of modern martial arts training. Included will be a history of the martial arts and a description of different styles and traditions. You will learn about formal instruction and how to choose a school for you or your children.

In part three, lessons 26-30, you will learn how to develop a confident attitude and manner that will deter bullies, abusers and criminals. You will investigate the psychological aspects of the martial arts that you can begin to use immediately to bring greater peace to your life. You will learn how to apply your newly acquired skills to all areas of your life as you become more productive at work and a responsible partner and parent at home.

All lessons include extensive links and annotated bibliographies to expand and continue your self-defense skill building. You do not need formal instruction or training to benefit from the important information in this course. You will learn how to develop your awareness, which is critical to your personal safety. For increased peace of mind, the time you invest in this course will be well spent.

Recommended time to complete: 3 hours per week for 10 weeks.

For a FREE sample lesson, go to MasterSuccess.com.

Tuition: $197.

ABOUT OUR PUBLICATIONS

The American Success Institute publishes a series of pocket-sized motivational quotebooks. Each book is illustrated and contains 365 quotes by a prominent person on topics related to successful living. Sample quotes from each book can be found on MasterSuccess.com. These books make excellent gifts or can be purchased and distributed by individuals or groups wishing to make a positive impact in their community. Corporations can use the books as incentive premiums. Customization is available for corporations ordering 2,000 or more books of a single title. Please call for details. Non-profit organizations can use the books for fundraising. Each year, several new titles will be added to this series. Please check our website for availability. Books may be purchased singly or in blocks of 50. Single copies are $6.00 and blocks of 50 are $150.00. Postage included.

Current titles:
- *Positive Mental Attitudes*
- *Positive Mental Attitudes II*
- *Tenga una actitud mental positiva (Spanish)*
- *African-Americans On Success*
- *Sports Legends On Success*
- *Women On Success*
- *101 Question and Answers On Small Business*
- *100 Action Principles Of The Shaolin*

To order online: MasterSuccess.com
To order by telephone: 1-800-585-1300
To order by mail: ASI, 5 North Main Street, Natick, MA 01760

International: Please order through Amazon.com or BN.com.

American Success Institute, Inc.

PLEASE JOIN US IN OUR WORK

The American Success Institute is a 501(c)3 nonprofit educational and publishing organization founded in 1993. ASI's teaching is done primarily through its books and two websites: MasterSuccess.com and Dojo.com. The mission of ASI is to foster positive values resulting in individual and societal peace and prosperity.

WE NEED YOUR HELP

Each year, ASI donates thousands of free motivational books through educational, correctional and social agencies. As you master success, we ask you to consider joining us in this work. You can purchase 50 book blocks of our pocket sized motivational quotebooks for $150 (postage included) and donate these books through non-profit organizations in your community. Non-profit organizations can purchase blocks of books for fundraising. If your company is involved in charitable giving, please ask them to consider our organization.

We need and appreciate individual donations in any amount. With a credit card, please call 1-800-585-1300 or make a donation to ASI on-line at MasterSuccess.com. Checks can be mailed to ASI at 5 North Main Street, Natick MA 01760. Donations are tax deductible. Please verify your particular tax situation with your accountant.

Thank you in advance for your help and generosity.

MASTER*SUCCESS*★com

The Master Success System extends far beyond the pages of this book. The operational center for the system is located at MasterSuccess.com. The site includes both multi-media enhancements and interactive capabilities. On-line additions and improvements are made every week. If you like the philosophy behind this book, you will certainly want to visit and bookmark MasterSuccess.com.

MasterSuccess.com will serve as a portal to Internet resources on all areas related to peace and prosperity, such as:

Personal finance	Real estate
Investments	Self-help
Exercise	Nutrition
Life sports	Self-defense
Leadership	Life enrichment
Personal style	Martial arts
Retirement	Entrepreneurship
General business	Peace
Government services	News and information
Education	Personal relationships

To assist you on your success journey, the site includes three in-depth tuition courses on small business, real estate and self-defense. Additional tuition courses are planned on a variety of subjects, including leadership, fitness, retirement and investment.

Dojo.com

Imagine that you have a kind uncle. You can go to him with your concerns, hopes and dreams. You know that he will listen and that his advice will always be supportive, non-judgmental and full of common sense. Your uncle is only interested in your success and happiness. He is the Shaolin Master.

Receive A Gift

Free T-Shirt Offer

Give A Gift

HELP US HELP YOU HELP OTHERS

SHARE
MASTER*SUCCESS*.com

Work with us to spread the positive message of Master Success and the Action Principles. Consider purchasing and giving copies of this book to friends, co-workers and loved ones. As with all our books, you may wish to donate copies through educational and social agencies in your community. Order on-line at MasterSuccess.com or by calling 1-800-585-1300. The price for the first copy of Master Success is always $19.95 and any number of other copies in the same order are $10.00 each. Postage is $5.00 for one copy and $2.00 for each additional copy. We suggest that International single orders be placed through Amazon.com or BN.com.

DELUXE AUDIO EDITIONS

Audio and CD version of Master Success

The complete unabridged versions of Master Success are available on CD or audiotape. Read by Bill FitzPatrick. A great way to reinforce the principles and concepts while you are driving or exercising. $79

Special Edition Shaolin Master CD

This limited edition CD features music composed for the Master Success project by the talented English composer Ivo Weisner. $16

INDEX

294